PROSTITUTION

PROSTITUTION
Recent and Unstoppable

IAN WALTERS

PARTRIDGE
A Penguin Random House Company

Print information available on the last page.

To order additional copies of this book, contact
Toll Free 800 101 2657 (Singapore)
Toll Free 1 800 81 7340 (Malaysia)
orders.singapore@partridgepublishing.com

www.partridgepublishing.com/singapore

Dedicated to

Marshall Sahlins

& to the memory of

Leslie White

CONTENTS

Acknowledgments.. ix

Chapter 1: Introduction 1

Chapter 2: Unstoppable Prostitution 16
            Entropy: a very brief introduction.....................18
            Shannon & information theory 20
            The theory of unstoppable prostitution: introduction.......22
            The species concept in sex work research.....................25
            Back to the theory 31
            Summary & Conclusions 38

Chapter 3: Recent Prostitution 41
            Fermi's dilemma.....................................46
            Prostitution in the historical & ethnographic record........47
            DMP societies......................................53
            VBH societies......................................56
            Set theory 58
            History as power series 66
            DMP to VBH & a measure of hierarchy 73
            A second prediction.................................76
            A hierarchy index..................................78
            A numerical example.................................81
            When does prostitution begin?
            1) Herodotus & history..............................91
            When does prostitution begin?
            2) hypothesis & prediction 101

Summary & Conclusions 108

Chapter 4: Implications of the theory 114

Drama after the Ice 116

Proposed causes 125

Intensification in the DMP 132

Linear transformations 136

Rogue Individuals 141

Collapse 151

White's energy relation 154

Summary & Conclusions 167

Chapter 5: Conclusions 170

References 177

Index 185

About the Author 187

Acknowledgments

Many thanks to all the wonderful sex workers in Vietnam, Cambodia, Thailand, Singapore and Australia (including Chinese, Malay, Japanese there) – as well as some on social media from all over - who have taught me so much about their industry and their lives.

I am grateful to Professor Fred Adams for providing me with an electronic offprint of his article cited.

Tong Phuoc Hung drew Figure 2.1 and Anna Willis drafted Figures 3.1 and 3.2 for me. Many thanks folks.

I have huge regard for many of my anthropological intellectual ancestors, my culture heroes, even though I never met any of them. I dedicate this book to the two most prominently involved in the ideas dealt with here. However, I am realistic enough to know that both would be disappointed in it – White not only for my upsetting of his energy harnessing (and therefore technological) determinism, but for daring to suggest individuals may have been responsible for the revolution, in the face of all-determining culture; Sahlins on the other hand, for my sell-out to (what he would see as) the rampant individualism of Hobbesian greed and Foulcauldian power. Both would abhor the minor amount of words I devote to symbolism. But it's not that simple. I know my symbols; and

I appreciate their power and place in history. And, I hope I satisfactorily acknowledge the cultural, the symbolic dimensions of the people and their histories I am dealing with, whether they be rogues or other.

In an interview which I am extremely grateful for having heard, the late great evolutionary biologist Stephen Jay Gould claimed an excellent volume for consultation on presentation was the US Army Training Manual. In that august publication Gould claimed, instructors were extolled to tell em what ya gunna tell em, then tell em, then tell em what ya told em. As my book is so short, and its theoretical arguments fairly succinct, the work runs the risk of sounding tediously repetitive when at beginnings and endings I set out respectively my aims and my conclusions. I hope Gould's take on the military's sound pedagogical advice gets me off the hook.

CHAPTER I

Introduction

In this book I present a theory of prostitution. Or at least, to the extent that prostitution may be considered as a variable which is a function of some other variable, the work is an examination of prostitution at the ends of that function. Which is another way of saying that I offer a theory for the beginning (one end) and what will be seen to be the non-termination of prostitution (other end). In an earlier book titled *Sex Work in Vietnam* (Walters 2013) I discussed the latter: the unstoppability of prostitution through history thus far, and into the foreseeable future.

When I was undertaking the analysis for Walters (2013) I could not fail to be impressed by the contradiction between, on the one hand, Vietnamese government claims that after reunification of the country in 1975 they had managed to eradicate prostitution, and on the other, the rampant prostitution that dominated vast precincts of Vietnamese urban and rural landscapes through the 1990s and early 2000s when my data had been collected. The sheer resilience of Vietnamese prostitution drew both my attention and my admiration. Of course I was sceptical of the government claims voiced repeatedly though their state-owned media, but I had no evidence to gainsay them or agree with them. If their claims were far-fetched, then I pondered what the situation might really have been. But then again, if they were right, or nearly so, I sat in awe of the above-mentioned resilience and ability to rebound and recover.

Then I read Gail Hershatter's (1997) great book. Coincidentally it turned out that the 1950s Chinese had made exactly the same claim for the onset of communist government. They too had eradicated prostitution. Yet they too, by the 1990s and early 2000s, lived in a world of vigorously practised prostitution (documented by ethnography, politics and sociology, as well as popular media). But unlike me, Hershatter had access to historical records for the critical period. She was able to show quite unmistakably that prostitution continued on under the new regime, albeit in altered and adapted forms, with lower public and social profile. It had not been eradicated at all.

I wondered if the Vietnamese horn blowing could be as false as the wild claims of their Chinese compatriots. I began to think along two lines, in tandem, in parallel. The first, empirical. Let's say the Vietnamese situation mirrored the Chinese. Then that spelled out behaviour of Vietnamese sex industry participants akin to that of their northern neighbours. Refusal to be driven down. Did these cases allow for wider generalisation? I began to think about the fascist regimes of modern times and their behaviour in regard to sex work: Hitler and Pol Pot came immediately to mind. In both those countries, for and after the reign of terror, prostitution returned and triumphed, adopting new strategies and tactics as well as returning to old. I thought about the inability of Western and other capitalist governments to abolish and eliminate prostitution: I had literature on Australia, the UK, the USA, Japan, and several Southeast Asian countries. There seemed to be a pattern: in the long term prostitution was unable to be stopped by politics and political force.

The second parallel line of thought concerned theory. As I had no data, and as historians of modern Vietnam appeared to hold little interest in prostitution as a social phenomenon, despite its key role in family and state economies (Walters 2013), I wondered if there was any theory that might help me. I searched around a bit, thinking of the kinds of phenomena that might generate appropriate theory.

Decades earlier as a student I had studied biological diversity, whose quantitative beginning centres around an index introduced by Claude Shannon. It derived essentially from Boltzmann's Law in statistical mechanics, and was applied via the information theory that Shannon virtually built up as a discipline by himself. The theory concerned the ability – given certain caveats - of a resilient signal to be transmitted through a noisy channel.

Here then was a theory I could apply. Shannon had proved such a signal was unstoppable, in the way that entropy – the quality of energy introduced through the Second Law of Thermodynamics – never fails to increase. I wrote down such a theory (see Endnotes to chapter 6 of Walters 2013). I re-visit that theory again here, hanging a few decorations on the previous version, elaborating it a little as well as setting it in place among other unstoppable phenomena.

The most prominent of these unstoppables is entropy, which is created, like many other physical phenomena, in or following the Big Bang origin of the universe. Or, to look at it another way, a subjective Cartesian homocentric way, it is created in the Second Law of Thermodynamics. The important point about unstoppable phenomena like entropy, or indeed like prostitution, is that once created, they will go on literally until the end of time, or at least in the case of prostitution, time involving dimensions of intelligent or human life.

Essentially that part of the theory says that no amount of effort devoted to abolition, proscription or criminalisation of prostitution will put an end to it. Or more formally, as I will show in chapter 2, it is unstoppable unless it isn't. This claim is not as contradictory as it may at first take seem. For it invokes the so-called Newtonian caveat – mentioned in Walters (2013) but not displayed formally there - which is deployed here as one of the new additions to the theory to make it fit more tightly with cosmological realities and planetary extinction probabilities. That is, prostitution is shown to be unstoppable up to all known human social and political limits, but of course will be affected by larger biological and cosmological events in future Earth and solar histories.

I also develop the idea of a beginning for prostitution, the other end of the function, and show that even though little can be unambiguously determined regarding exact dates and places, there are a few relevant and important theoretical remarks that can be made. These follow from the prehistoric, historic and anthropological data available. The first and second of these claims reject popular and prevalent notions of prostitution having been with us always, along with the view that it has some mythological status as the oldest profession. Already in Walters (2013) I have, in an argument of some length, dismissed the idea of it constituting the oldest profession. Here I suggest some other quite useful things which can be said about its recent beginnings; things that link the anthropological and historic past with contemporary and future cultures and societies.

In chapter 3 I make the case for its recent origin. This brushes up against the historical and archaeological evidence, as I just said, scant though this is. Because that evidence is thin on the ground, any attempted theory is forced to push away into the territory of conjecture. But there's nothing new in that, and archaeologists and ancient historians will not fear it.

On the other hand, one conjecture which grows out of a hypothesis I presented in Walters (2013) concerning prostitution's role in the origins of what may be called bedroom sex, does lead us to possible testability. Provided, that is, archaeologists are prepared to a) accept the veracity of some ancient textual history and social commentary, principally but not only, from Herodotus; and b) be willing to devote time and energy to the operationalisation of some key variables from their field surveys and excavations. If these incorporate sufficient flexibility in a manner reminiscent of bending and stretching, they should allow researchers to make a few leaps of faith, whence testing my claims becomes possible. In a nutshell these claims are simply that prostitution begins as a Holocene phenomenon associated with so-called complex societies (civilization), and there is a possibility that untested conjectures in the more popular literature which link prostitution to temples, hold some interest. At the very least my ideas and suggestions should provide food for future thought, and perhaps for future field and laboratory work.

Hierarchy has featured in all discussions of these Holocene societies. In the theory I derive this as a key causal variable. I argue that it is more productive to see hierarchy not just as an attribute of social life in these complex Holocene societies, but as a property which can be deployed to look at social change more generally. That is, I suggest the anthropological adage that all societies have hierarchy as a key property of their social organisation (even if that hierarchy is only minimally revealed through sex and age). To allow calculations of hierarchy in any given society I present an index for it. I give a simplified numerical example to show how this might work.

And that's the end of the theory. Short and sweet. But, the central ideas I develop will allow us to move forward from prostitution, as it were, to consider implications for several major and long standing issues concerning origins and developmental histories of the so-called complex societies of the Holocene. These should at the very least hold interest for archaeologists, anthropologists and ancient historians who otherwise might care not a chit for prostitution as an academic topic.

In chapter 4 I discuss three of these implications in terms of the ideas developed in my theory: hypotheses for the origins of complex societies; ideas about the longevity and outcomes (i.e. collapse) of many or most of these ancient societies; and finally Leslie White's well known energy and culture relation concerning social evolution. Strictly speaking, like ecological systems (May 1978), human societies or social systems do not evolve. This is because natural selection acts mostly on individuals or groups of related individuals. Societies in that sense, and along with them cultures, cannot be regarded as units subject to Darwinian evolution. Having said that, societies do change over time; they have histories. Hence we need not adhere to the hard neo-Darwinian line, as there are other forces of influence in evolution. What is more, descent with modification aptly describes what goes on in culture and society over time. However, it will be useful to remember that such histories are driven by forces that are political and cultural; not by the forces of nature or the physical environment.

Let me say a bit more about these implications, briefly opening the topic as it were, for further and later development in chapter 4. What used to be termed civilization has been on the minds of Europeans since the expansion of mercantile capitalism clattered, in shock and awe, up against the rich histories, cultures, and living societies encountered in other parts of the world. Thus early archaeologists, Egyptologists, historians, even Mr Marx, all had their ideas about how it was and why it was these ancient societies that left such stunning material records, or alternatively the tattered bloody remains of christian conquest, came about. In addition, nineteenth century anthropologists adventurously came up with various schemes that attempted to set all this amid a context of the new Darwinian notions spreading with such vigour among social thinkers of the time. These nineteenth century theories evoked the idea of a single developmental pathway for all mankind involving several stages through which their evolving societies must pass on the way to a monogamous scientific christian European glory.

Then in the twentieth century, after abandoning nineteenth century evolution by unilinear stages, thinkers from various disciplines came up with a set of theories or conjectures about the determinants of these origins. Most of these were mechanistic, involving as causal forces such things as intensive agriculture needing construction and management of large irrigation systems, territorial circumscription, warfare, population growth, and agricultural intensification itself (which included factors related to population, climate and technology).

But according to recent reviews of the subject, none of the ideas – we may call them theories though none are technically or logically derived – concerning the origins of complex societies, alone and unaided stand the test of data fit. As hypotheses they obviously also fail, for the very same reason. At risk of deep offence to Messrs Tylor, Morgan, Spencer, et al., much less Messrs Childe, Carneiro, Wittfogel, et al. from the twentieth century, it is probably better to refer to them as conjectures, a term which captures the perception, insight and inference entailed in all of them, but does not offend the sensibilities of those who demand more rigour and data compatibility in the arena of evidential examination. This is discussed in more detail in the first part of chapter 4.

Many ancient complex societies collapsed, either under their own metaphoric weight, or due to external circumstances impinging upon them. Christians and conquistadors were not the only barbarians at the gate. Many authors have written and speculated on this issue, either generally or for particular societies. None to my knowledge have built in to derived theory a consideration of the possibility of collapse that arises out of the mechanics of the very origins of these social forms. I show how my theory can be deployed to this end. The theory for origins presented here contains within itself the high likelihood that the modal outcome for such social forms will eventually be their demise. Which is another way of saying that collapse emerges from this theory of origins as a prediction. This is the second of the theoretical implications presented in chapter 4.

Finally in that chapter, I address the famous relation due to Leslie White, that energy capture is the engine of what he called society, product (of goods and services), cultural development, cultural advancement, or social progress. The nineteenth century European thinkers mentioned earlier were equally enamoured of the idea of progress, judging it to have not only a reality, but a scientific usefulness. White delicately followed their lead. He suggested that energy capture together with the efficiency with which it is utilised, gave us a measure of this product. That is

$$E \times T \rightarrow P$$

where P measures what he initially termed product, but actually implies cultural advancement or social progress, E is energy harnessed in any given society, and T a measure of the efficiency with which such energy is utilised.

Many in the twentieth century academic world railed against this, not least for its unoperationalised nineteenth century dependent variable. These scholars dismissed social progress as being something that measures nothing more than an idea of closeness to us, that is, to nineteenth century

European-ness (or its twentieth century hangovers). White's relation has thus rightly fallen out of favour. Nevertheless, after abandoning progress, many thinkers remain fetched by the idea of a correlation between some idea of social change over time with the amount of energy that various societies harness and use. As do I.

I think our great White was onto something. But as I will show in chapter 4, he didn't go far enough, that's all. He bet on a losing thing: a subjective ethnocentric progress. As I just said, this would not long after be shown to have no serious value in scientific thinking. However, in later decades of the twentieth century, attempts to rescue White's idea while watering down allusions to a racist, ethnocentric, political notion of progress have resulted in newer softer terms for any such variables put forward. Hence my reference above to the contemporary deployment of this term social evolution, as a substitute for White's original and more loaded dependent variable. More on that anon.

I turn again to hierarchy as a key player here. I make an attempt to use the notion of hierarchy as I derive it in the theory, to see what assistance it can provide in thinking more about White's insight. For I think we have to acknowledge that despite the dud idea of progress, he was at least in the ballpark, as Americans are wont to say, with his claim that energy is somehow involved. He was the one investigator who nominated energy as a variable of interest, and that alone, I think, is sufficient to warrant some kind of appeal for a re-trial; further exploration of his idea: where and how energy fits into this picture of rapidly changing Holocene societies.

However, the result I present in this part of chapter 4 is contra-White, it is surprising, and it may even appear counterintuitive to some anthropological or archaeological readers nurtured on White-like thinking. In fact it will quite possibly shock such archaeologists and anthropologists, possibly historians, and perhaps even an odd sociologist, especially those who work in and around the field of these so-called complex societies as they change and develop through to historic and contemporary times. Put simply the result is this: energy is there alright as a relevant term, but in the key relation linking it to social change, it appears as a dependent variable.

Energy, in this new consideration, is not the important force driving whatever might substitute as an acceptable replacement for social progress (terms such as social evolution). Rather it is a measurable dependent variable which is a function of hierarchy. The last part of chapter 4 provides the details.

The final chapter is a very short foray through a set of conclusions. There I emphasise again the unstoppability of prostitution. In addition, as I stated above, by the empirical evidence as it now stands, prostitution is a Holocene phenomenon, an attribute of what are commonly termed complex societies. Up till now in this introduction I have gone along with that term in order that readers are immediately aware of as well as relaxed and comfortable with the concept I am referring to. But I alert readers here, as I remind them in the conclusions, that throughout this book I suggest a generalisation of this term; one which, while at first sounding equally vague, actually carries more precision: Very Big Hierarchy (VBH) societies.

The conclusions remind the reader that the notion of VBH societies can be given quantitative definition, related to hierarchy (initially this is shown in chapter 3). Apart from one suggestion by Gregory Johnson and Henry Wright (e.g. Johnson 1987; Wright 1987; discussed in Wenke 1999:406-408) that complex societies can be considered as those which have at least three observable levels of administrative hierarchy, as far as

I can tell this is something that has never before occurred in discussions of civilization and complex societies. And it is this which leads directly to the implications introduced above.

It is civilization that gave us prostitution. And while it may seem oddly askew at first glance, it is a discussion of the origins of prostitution that present us here with the opportunity to cast some light on larger issues of social and political history and structural change in cultures.

This book and its theory fit within that school of thought that stresses the need to consider social, cultural, historical and political factors as central when looking for causality in the rise of VBH societies. I derive a key causal variable: hierarchy. I argue for another variable that makes it all happen: the Rogue Individual (RI). Finally as briefly outlined above, I summarise the implications of the theory for the above three issues concerned with the rise and demise of VBH societies and the energy they harness.

Returning briefly to the second sentence of this Introduction, let me elaborate on the major thematic technique I intend to use throughout the work. This is the method of functions. For our purposes a variable y is said to be a function of a variable x if for each value of x we obtain a corresponding value in y. We write this $y = f(x)$, which reads y equals f of x, meaning y is a function of x. For example, if $y = 2x$ we know from this function that it turns any positive whole number x which is not already even, into an even number y. Simmons (1996:1) has called the notion of function the "master concept of the exact sciences." He also claimed it to be "the most important concept in all of mathematics" (Simmons 1996:22). Hardy ([1908] 2008:40) had told us as much a hundred years ago: "This notion of functional dependence of one variable upon another is perhaps the most important in the whole range of higher mathematics." While I do not pretend for one moment that social sciences have attained or can attain the status of the exact sciences, the notions of dynamic variables and the method of functions prove quite useful tools to study some of the key ideas of social and cultural change.

It has become fashionable in the literature related to the particular changes in human society discussed in this book, to move away from the theory of functions, to call upon some aspect of mathematical ideas about discontinuity. Discussions of both the rise of so-called complex societies as well as their demise, or collapse, have tended in recent years to deploy notions related to what is known as singularity theory, or as I said, through its ideas of discontinuity, or of catastrophe. Rene Thom (1989 [1972]) originated much of the thinking that has been taken up by biologists, archaeologists, sociologists and others in dealing with this and similar issues. Coming to terms with – or in my case struggling to come to terms with – this form of theoretical thinking has has not been easy. For theories of this type move sharply away from comfortable analysis, the theory of continuous functions, that has characterised classical quantitative modelling (Thom 1989:9).

For 300 sublime years classical quantitative modelling gave us answers to almost every significant theoretical discovery made in the hard sciences. Only quantum mechanics brought a disorder that would not be shoe-horned by analysis. And of course, then came these rich ideas of Rene Thom. However, despite all this, as the frontiers of theory moved elsewhere - and population ecology is where I become familiar with it - classical quantitative modelling still found a rich vein of ideas with which to sophisticate ecological, and then general biological, thinking. Initially through Verhulst, Lotka and Volterra, then in more recent times, especially the 1970s, with names like Hutchinson, Macarthur and May in the van, these classical theories using continuous models produced first class insights for ecology. See Hutchinson (1978) for a beautiful introduction to these.

However, through the 1970s a parallel development, largely centred on the empirical field data relating to very complex population dynamics, began to question the adequacy of standard theories developed using continuous functions. This work, due largely but not entirely to C.S.Holling, has now grown into the key research area known as resilience theory (see Scheffer 2009; Gunderson, Allen & Holling 2010; Holling 2010a, 2010b, 2010c; Ludwig, Jones & Holling 2010). But the mathematics required for appropriate theory in this area involves formal rather than continuous models, details catastrophes and discontinuities, is often difficult, and much remains undiscovered - as Thom told us all those decades ago (Thom 1989, Arnold 2004). In fact, where theory has been applied most successfully is often in approaches that remain initiated in the comfortable mathematics of analysis, which is to say continuous models, albeit with catastrophe cusps and such things, built in to them (e.g. Ludwig, Jones & Holling 2010).

In the empirical world addressed by social sciences and humanities, such recognition of complexity (and singularities) is of course, basally necessary. In my own field, anthropology, is it especially so. Yet over the past century or more we see many an anthropologist grappling with the theoretical issues which captured their interest, reaching out towards mathematical endeavours, yet shackled by (presumably) limited skill sets or uninterested audiences. We see Levi-Strauss, possibly the greatest of them all, using mathematical metaphors and logic throughout his writings. Radcliffe-Brown went so far as to deploy mathematical terms such as domain and range in areas of his originality. The great Leslie White used the most simple algebra in his attempts to characterise cultural change and its causes. Then right on through to the maligned

American functionalist materialism (Marvin Harris and many others) there is this stance which continues with the insistence that there can be a science of culture and society (which must, by definition, include somewhere a deference to mathematical thinking).

I am attempting here another step in this direction: searching for answers to important questions using mathematical theory. In fact I venture to suggest the book is an entrée into what might loosely be termed mathematical history. Or perhaps more correctly, if I may be allowed, as another attempt to put anthropology at the centre of history (Sahlins 2000:527). As you will see, the empirical evidence (and the questions) derive from cultural anthropology, ethnography, archaeology, ancient history and classics. But the mathematics remains rudimentary, set in the ways of classical continuous quantitative modelling. However, this is possibly highly appropriate, as it turned out to be for much of population biology in the period 1950-1980.

In this book, except for some basic points made here in my Introduction by Thom (1989) and Arnold (2004), I avoid singularity theory with its discontinuities and catastrophes. There are two reasons for this. Firstly, as theory travelled across various disciplinary frontiers – and I again fall back on the example of population ecology here – classical continuous quantitative models proved, even in extreme cases like those worked on by Holling and others, to provide useful and productive insights (again as e.g.: Ludwig, Jones & Holling 2010). Thus might it hopefully prove in social studies.

Secondly, as I intimated, the mathematics brought to us by Thom and others – for example, differential and algebraic geometry and differential topology (Arnold 2004:6) - is exceedingly abstract and difficult (see for example Clark 1984; Mendelson 1990). These remain at this stage – and possibly forever – beyond the likes of me. Perhaps, to cast a positive note, by next book I may have mastered a little more of them. But for now, as you will see, since I have kept my questions simple, classical continuous analysis stands us in pretty good stead as I attempt to account for the phenomena under discussion.

Finally, a technical point regarding my mode of presentation. The book is so short it would seem a waste of time and space to make use of footnotes or endnotes. Should I attempt to ease the pain for readers by hiding mathematical rigour in endnotes – as I did in *Sex Work in Vietnam* – there would be almost no main text to the book. So at behest of that, everything happens in the one narrative. However, the read, both the theory I set out herein, as well as its implications, is in some part mathematical. Be warned about and prepared for that. Nevertheless, I try my best to characterise what is happening in fairly simple clear English, hoping that all readers, regardless of their levels of mathematical competence or fear, will be able to cope with most of it. At least you'll get the gist. And when you do, some of it may even amuse.

CHAPTER 2

Unstoppable Prostitution

In this chapter I re-visit the theory of unstoppable prostitution first developed in *Sex Work in Vietnam* (Walters 2013). It is my claim, and the outcome of that theory, that prostitution is what I term an unstoppable phenomenon. That is, it is a phenomenon which, once begun, created or developed, continues unabated despite any efforts or forces assembled to stop it. In other words, now that we have prostitution on the planet, according to the theory, it will continue through to the end, ceasing only when we or our descendant equivalent beings go extinct, or the Earth itself ceases to exist.

Prostitution is an unstoppable idea. It is one of those phenomena whose best known examples are probably entropy, viruses, both biological and computer, war and Very Big Hierarchy (VBH) societies. These are phenomena that while neither inevitable nor necessary (in some functionalist way of progress or advancement), take on momenta of their own once they do arise, once circumstances bring about their origins. Such phenomena have their origins in the means and mode of production, perhaps contradictions in those, combined with the luck or fortune to be in the right place at the right time (or is that wrong place at the wrong time?) when fortuitous circumstances were lurking. They can be metaphorised as akin to the products of biological mutation, especially those of the opportunistic kind. For while they are well behaved in terms of the laws of nature as we know them, they possess attributes of growth, often potentially rapid growth, and if applicable, for example, self-reproductivity, short generation time, virile fecundity. These are cascading, almost free-wheeling, resilient properties that defy all social, political and technological attempts to thwart them.

While we burn resources in order to develop vaccines and firewalls, really all we can do is hold back the tide a while, like the communist authorities in 1950s China or post-1975 Vietnam (see Walters 2013), by resorting to prostitute imprisonment, assassination, or whatever else it took. But once the jackboots – be they viral drugs, security programs or prosticide - come off the metaphorical necks, the unstoppable phenomena let loose as before. Thirty years without visible prostitution in communist China, thirteen years in communist Vietnam (Walters 2013), are but blips in the great warps of historical and universal time and the worldlines of unstoppable phenomena. By the late 1980s or even a little earlier, prostitution bounced back in both Chinese and Vietnamese jurisdictions, with a vengeance as it were. Why? Because it is unstoppable, that's why.

I am not the first to reach this conclusion about prostitution. Goodall (1995) in a work unknown to me when I wrote *Sex Work in Vietnam*, makes the claim various times in the introductory part of his book. For example: "the abolition of prostitution ... is incapable of ever being achieved in a free society" (p.xvii); "prostitution is ineradicable" (p.2); "prostitution is always going to be an essential element of the human condition" (p.2); "We have never been able to get rid of prostitutes and never will" (p.3); "... prostitution has continued unabated up to the present time, it is fair to assume that it will continue to persist in the future" (p.15). However, it should be noted that said claims are only that; no data are produced and most certainly no theory presented to support the claims. Nevertheless, it is comforting to find another author who draws the same conclusion as I obtain in the theory developed both in Walters (2013) and this present volume, from the broad-sweep empirical evidence of multicultural history that confronts us.

By way of an introduction to unstoppable phenomena, I begin this chapter with an extremely brief cavort through a background of perhaps the most famous and important unstoppable phenomenon. So central is it in fact, that there are laws of nature out of which it arises and is described, and for what catastrophe coincides with it were it ever to be stopped (the attainment of absolute zero temperature). This is entropy.

Other unstoppables are mentioned above, including two forms of viruses. Cultural forms such as war and especially VBH societies will form a large part of the discussion in the remainder of the book post-chapter 2.

Entropy: a very brief introduction

In classical thermodynamics, the concept of entropy is defined by the second law of thermodynamics, which states that the entropy of an isolated system always increases or remains constant (http://en.wikipedia. org/wiki/Entropy) in the course of spontaneous change. Mathematically, this is given by the following relation:

$$dS \geq 0 \qquad\qquad (2.1)$$

where S is the entropy and the differential dS gives a measure of an infinitesimal amount of that entropy.

For isolated systems, (2.1) tells us that entropy never decreases. This fact has several important consequences in science and technology:

first, it prohibits perpetual motion machines; and second, it implies the unfolding of entropy has the same directionality as, and hence gives to us, the arrow of time. Increases in entropy correspond to irreversible changes in a system (http://en.wikipedia.org/wiki/Entropy). In its original formulation, as determined by the second law, entropy is seen as a fundamental thermodynamic property that characterizes the quality of energy (Atkins 2010).

In thermodynamics, entropy can only be known empirically, whereas in that branch of physics known as statistical mechanics, it is a function of the distribution of the system on its micro-states (http://en.wikipedia.org/wiki/Statistical_thermodynamics). In the latter, entropy is essentially a measure of the number of ways in which a system may be arranged, often taken to be a measure of disorder (the higher the entropy, the higher the disorder). Specifically this definition describes entropy as being proportional to the logarithm of the number of possible microscopic configurations of the individual atoms and molecules of the system (microstates) which could give rise to the observed macroscopic state (macrostate) of the system. The constant of proportionality is the Boltzmann constant.

For a given set of variables, entropy measures the degree to which the probability of the system is spread out over different possible microstates. The more such states available to the system, the greater the entropy. That is,

$$S = k \log W \qquad (2.2)$$

where as before S is entropy, W the number of ways a system can be arranged to express its energy (microstates), and k is the constant, named after Ludwig Boltzmann who first discussed these ideas in the nineteenth century.

The Boltzmann law (2.2) tells us that entropy is the degree of randomness or disorder in any system. Entropy is Enlightenment science's original and most powerful unstoppable phenomenon. It is one way traffic to the end. And the second law (2.1) tells us that.

Sir Arthur Eddington, who among other things did the measurements confirming the prediction of Einstein's general theory of relativity that light waves from the distant stars would be bent in the gravitational field of the sun, claimed that the "law that entropy always increases – the second law of thermodynamics – holds, I think, the supreme position among the laws of Nature." (quoted by Shannon & Weaver 1998:12.) Peter Atkins (2010:xii) calls the second law "one of the all-time great laws of science," as it "illuminates why anything … happens at all."

Shannon & information theory

So, as we have just seen, the second law of thermodynamics states in its simplest form that entropy always increases (see 2.1 above). What follows relies heavily on that. It is also reliant upon information theory and the manner in which it owes its key notions to entropy and the second law.

Following the Boltzmann law, Shannon utilized the notion of disorder to deploy entropy in the theory of information transmission he developed around the time of World War II. The greater the uncertainty in a message, the greater disorder, the greater diversity (in the sense now applied in ecology), the greater the entropy. For diversity is inherently linked to the fundamental principle of entropy (Wurtz & Annila 2008).

More specifically in such cases the entropy is a logarithmic measure of the density of microstates. Consider this alternate version of (2.2):

$$H = -k \sum p_i \log p_i$$

(2.3)

where k is as before the Boltzmann constant, p_i is the probability of the system to be in the ith microstate, and H measures information or diversity. Since the introduction of this index a plethora of diversity indices have been developed (see Magurrin 2004).

In addition, entropy and information can be linked in other ways. Karnani, Paakkonen & Annila (2009:2159) show that the rate of entropy increase can be written in terms of information flow as the Boltzmann constant times the rates of message (information) flow times the ratio of free energy to average energy. Then, as the second law states that $dS/dt \geq 0$, this product must also be ≥ 0.

Which is to say

$$\frac{dS}{dt} = k \sum \frac{dN}{dt} \left[\left(\sum \mu_k + \Delta Q - \mu_j \right) / kT \right] \geq 0$$

where N here represents information, ΔQ is external energy, and μ_k and μ_j are potentials associated with the physical character of the information. The numerator in parentheses represents the potential energy differences, and the entire bracket the energy ratio already referred to above (free to average) (Karnani, Paakkonen & Annila 2009:2158).

This equation "clarifies that emergence of a nested hierarchical data structure of 'messages within messages' is a probable evolutionary scenario. For example, a genome contains chromosomes that, in turn, are composed of gene regulatory networks, which house genes written by codons that are made of bases" (Karnani, Paakkonen & Annila 2009:2161). In other words, the equation predicts a taxonomy. Such an organisation of information "is a natural outcome, as it results from evolution towards the free energy minimum state" (Karnani, Paakkonen

& Annila 2009:2161). In fact, it's not only natural; Swenson and Turvey (1991) call such an order production "inexorable."

It is easily seen from the above, therefore, that when energy, information and entropy are thought about in this way, taxonomic hierarchies follow naturally. This is useful for what follows, in the sense that I deploy a taxonomy as a tool to aid thinking about prostitution in a quantitative way. I could have done that without such a logical development, or indeed prediction, as I did earlier in Walters (2013), but it helps to see some theoretical justification for what I have chosen to do.

The theory of unstoppable prostitution: introduction

The theory relies on the notion of the validity of a taxonomy of prostitution as initially developed in chapter 4 of Walters (2013) to help account for changes in what I referred to in that previous work as the temporary wife cycle. Temporary wives are women who move in with men for a relatively short time (say for a week on up to a year or two), providing them with sexual and domestic services in return for payment of money or materiel. From my own experience they are very common in contemporary Asia (Walters 2013), and no doubt in most other parts of the modern world as well (or at least the third world anyhow). They were recorded historically by people working on the texts relating to the Early Modern period in Southeast Asia (Reid 1993a, 1993b; Andaya 1998), where the temporary wives were local women who assisted visiting foreign men: businessmen and merchants, bureaucrats and colonial officials, sea captains and the like.

The historians of Early Modern Southeast Asia considered temporary wives to be a different social state from that of prostitution. In fact they clearly demarcated between the two in their discussions. They saw in this a change in moral values over time, from temporary wives (approved and condoned) to prostitution (disapproved of), as states developed, money economies were introduced, and influences such as proselytising christianty took hold. In Walters (2013) I dismissed the former idea, disagreeing that temporary wives were in fact anything but another form of prostitution (thereby calling into question the latter claim as well – it may of course be valid, but not for the reasons they claimed). I was able to do this because of the results of an ethnographic study I had undertaken of contemporary temporary wives in Vietnam. The women who undertook these activities were invariably prostitutes who, instead of moving from one temporary wife situation to another as their male benefactors came and went, moved with such departures into another form of prostitution (which for simplicity of nomenclature I called whoring) as they sought a newcomer to whom they could attach as a temporary wife once more. From travels, though not formal study, I now know this occurs in contemporary times across a far broader front than just Vietnam.

Further, by developing a taxonomy I was able to show that in fact temporary wives could be seen to have the same status (taxonomically) as girlfriends, whores, and other kinds of sex workers, the terms for which I gathered together into a category I named prostitute (or sex worker). This gives far greater analytical freedom to the idea of temporary wives, makes that category less restrictive, and suggests the taxonomy which provides further insights into how sex work is organised in its labile, dynamic, protean forms, both now and in the past. That is, I found women who moved easily and often between categories, being a temporary wife as long as it lasted, then becoming a bar girl for a while, or a waitgirl, or a karaoke girl, etc. Temporary wife was simply one more version of prostitution.

This notion was further advanced in chapter 6 of Walters (2013), with the hierarchy being upgraded to a 3-level taxonomy. When coupled with the most simple measure of diversity this idea could be usefully deployed to characterise the range of prostitution in different historical periods. I gave examples from both Vietnam and China, the former being my own research data and the latter taken from Gail Hershatter's magnificent (1997) volume on early twentieth century prostitution in Shanghai. As preliminaries, the theory required acceptance of two basic conditions. The first is that descriptors of diversity in such evolutionary phenomena involve multiplicative factors, which in turn implies that the natural variables of discussion will be logarithmic (May 1975; MacArthur 1975; Walters 2013). The second is that in any given social and historical situation there will exist an upper bound number of prostitution taxa, say A, which is determined by historical, cultural, and political determinants abroad at the time. We define an upper bound as follows.

If S is a non-empty set of real numbers,

a real number x is called an upper bound for S if $x \geq s$ for all $s \in S$ where s is an element of set S.

While a real number x is a least upper bound for S if x is an upper bound for S and $x \leq y$ for every upper bound y of S. This means that technically A is a least upper bound.

The first key theoretical point that follows from these requirements is that any measure for the evolution of prostitution particular to any era in any given social context will be some fraction of A, less than or equal to it.

So, I seek a system description which involves both the notion of a taxonomy involving the species concept and a diversity measure such as (2.3), together with the idea of an upper bound in the number of these species. But what do I mean by species? We are talking about prostitution after all. Let me digress a little to explain what I mean. I will show briefly that if I am allowed to introduce a species notion into considerations of prostitution, the rewards are such that I am able to use taxonomy, information theory and entropy to produce a theory of unstoppable prostitution which fits all known factual evidence.

The species concept in sex work research

Many great ideas in Enlightenment science, historical and cultural scholarship have come about as direct result of the invention of some theoretical entity that acts as a springboard for the practical outcomes and consequences in the advancement of those ideas. The concept of infinity combined with the notion of things in some limit becoming vanishingly, infinitesimally small, allowed us to have a calculus that put men on the moon and returned them safely to Earth. The invention of zero as a mathematical entity, among many other things, allowed development of the binary codes that let me sit at keyboard and type this manuscript, then send it electronically to my editor, after which some of you can read it via the online version. Culture, a notion we still have no agreed and fixed definition of, has nevertheless allowed deep insights into the way learning and social norms shape individual and group behaviour across the vast span of human existence.

In this chapter I introduce one such theoretical entity with which I can put forth various practical and historically significant measures that potentially bring benefits for sex work and sex workers. It is the species concept, well known and utilized in biology, that I claim is useful to sex work research. Or at least a modified species concept, one vastly different from the biological species concept, but constructed along similar lines via taxonomies. This may sound a bit vague, but to serve my purposes I will describe a concept that is surprisingly flexible yet sufficiently rigid to be quantitatively useful. As I showed in Walters (2013) such quantitative usefulness then leads directly in certain cases I discussed, to testable theory.

There is no delusion here that we can equate such a species concept with the quite firm notion used in biological evolution. What I have in mind is something far more fluid. There are no equivalents to capacity for successful reproduction, a bounded breeding group, the survival of fertile offspring, and so on. This species concept is much more fuzzy, but useful nonetheless. While the biological concept fences individual organisms in to a particular category, the concept I have in mind depends on categories with gated fences, so that individuals can move freely between one category and another. Individuals are born into biological species, live in them, reproduce in them, die in them, and sometimes fossilise in them. But here, there is nothing equivalent to saying individual sex worker I_i belongs in species P_i, as a lifelong or career long category. In a five year working career, say, any given sex worker might be a street walker, a brothel worker, a call girl, a girlfriend, a temporary wife, and a karaoke girl. Six species represented in one career (lifetime) as a sex worker. These can be at different stages of a career, one following the other, or even contemporaneous, such as a brothel worker who moonlights, once she returns home from her shift at the brothel, as a call girl.

In considerations of the biological world, species as bounded breeding entities are grouped together according to similarities. That is, according to attributes shared. We humans, for example, carry vast differences physically and mentally, and in personality and behaviour. Yet our shared DNA, reproductive biology and other features allow us to interbreed successfully. That is, to produce viable offspring, as members of the same species. Should Anglo Saxon Lord Highfalutin breed with a Jamaican slavegirl of Afro origins, the result will be a human baby. Should a native American from Tierra del Fuego breed with a Hmong girl from the uplands of Laos, result: the same. We are all in this together. Each and every one of us are members of the species *Homo sapiens*.

And what is more, our species, like all other biological species, is bounded, fenced in. Should Lord Highfalutin try to breed with his terrier, the results will not only not be a human baby, but will actually produce no outcome at all. That is, we cannot produce viable offspring when attempting breeding with members of other species. Occasional cross-breeds like mules (horse with donkey) or ligers (lion with tiger) do occur, but the offspring they produce are not reproductively viable. They are living dead ends. Because their parental species are bounded reproductively.

At one level this is the case with prostitution. Street walkers are street walkers no matter their locale of work, their age, their targeted clientele, or the language and currency they use in transactions. Bar girls are bar girls the world over. As are brothel girls. And, I emphasise again, temporary wives. Members of each of these categories share attributes with each other that they may not share with members of other categories. Street girls work in streets, bar girls in bars, etc. These species are bounded too, at least at that elementary level. The key differences here are that individual biological species members are, as I said above, born into and die in categories, Individual prostitutes may move in a day, a week, a year, a career, from one category to another, then another, and so on, as circumstances and whim demand. The categories are not fenced, but gated. The individual members are able to switch, to relocate, to alter behaviours. So at all levels above and beyond the basic, the kind of species concept I am advocating here for prostitution shows no boundedness whatsoever.

The idea of a taxonomy lets us group species together into other categories. These groupings of various closely related species are called genera (singular: genus). In similar fashion groups of closely related genera are grouped together into families. For example, biological taxonomists call our domestic cats by the Linnaean species name *Felis catus*. (The Swedish taxonomist Carl Linnaeus was the originator of this system, which he developed in his famous tome of 1735 – and many subsequent editions - titled *Systema Naturae*, The System of Nature.) Domestic cats are closely related to other cats such as the wildcat *Felis silvestris* and the Chinese mountain cat *Felis bieti*. These in turn are all related to other forms such as the lynx, for example the Canadian lynx *Lynx canadensis* and the bobcat *Lynx rufus*. And again all are relatives of the far larger and more ferocious lion *Panthera leo* and tiger *Panthera tigris*. Notice that we have three genera of cats here, each with its own particular species. They in turn are all members of the Family Felidae.

We can usefully deploy such a taxonomic hierarchy in discussions of sex worker categories. In Walters (2013) I suggested various species of sex work could be grouped together in the category (genus) whore, and it in turn could be lumped with other genera into a family level taxon which I termed prostitute (or sex worker). Such a technique allows us to bring into focus certain ideas which prove useful for examination of historical changes in sex work profiles and services.

Let me provide as example the case I introduced above. In Walters (2013) I discussed the notion of temporary wife, as introduced into the prostitution literature by historians of the Early Modern period in Southeast Asia. I presented seven case studies from contemporary Vietnam which show the continuity of this phenomenon into present times. But what do we mean by a temporary wife? Recall that this is a girl who meets up with a foreign man who arrives to do business for a period, moves in under the same roof with him, providing him sexual services and some degree of domestic care, possibly even assisting him in his business, or if she is experienced enough, with interpretation and translation. In return the foreigner provides for her during their liaison, and rewards her financially, with either money (later) or in earlier historical times before money came into use, goods and gifts and materiel. As I said earlier, the historians Reid (1993a, 1993b) and Andaya (1998) saw it as a category distinct from a prostitute, whence they described the transitions between, to and from, temporary wifedom and prostitution. I built on this (Walters 2013), interpreting temporary wifedom as merely another form of prostitution, not distinct from it. A new theory emerged from this claim which led to a prediction that consequently emerged from the new theory suggesting that periods of what I termed whoredom would be found to occur for any given Early Modern Southeast Asian sex worker between her sessions as temporary wife. This prediction is testable by further historical research.

My development of this key notion due to the historians depended upon viewing the situation differently from them. It requires thinking in the fluid manner I suggested above for types of sex work. That is, prostitute and temporary wife are not different categories in the way the historians used them. We can see it instead as one being a subset of the other: temporary wife is one type of prostitute. If we take prostitution as a catch-all category consisting in this first instance of temporary wives, whores, girlfriends (a particular Vietnamese-using-English term for a longish relationship that involves money transactions), street walkers, brothel workers, etc., we have begun to develop a taxonomy for sex work. Within such a taxonomy, each category (such as the examples just given) can be seen as species. In such a simple taxonomy, prostitution would be equivalent to a genus containing the species listed above. In Walters (2013) I suggested a 3-level taxonomy involving prostitute being equivalent to a family level category with various genera each potentially containing species made up of individual sex workers. To the most simple and useful of these genera I gave the name whore, a genus which then contained the various listed species (see Figure 2.1 below).

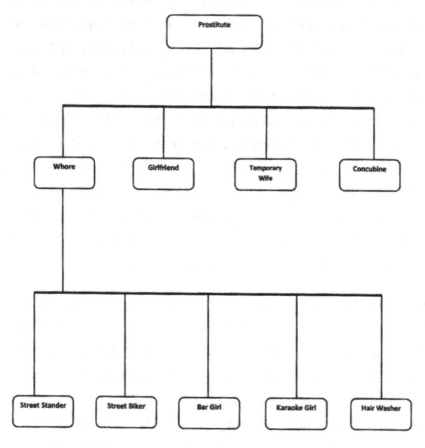

Figure 2.1. A 3-level taxonomy of prostitution.

Why am I doing this? What's it all about? The usefulness of the species concept comes in giving us a way to measure the diversity of sex work in any given context or situation. And that in turn proves not only useful, but essential to the development of productive theory and the predictions we can make from it. This is not about labels; it is not about one sex worker joking with another that she is a call girl, while you – she says to her friend – are a what? Reply: an effing street walker, you slut! No, it's not about that. For each given sex worker, as I say again for emphasis, can and usually will change species various times in a career or even during any given working day or night. Nobody has to be defined or labelled or pigeon holed. Nobody has to be fenced in. Nobody has to be stereotyped. The categories are the things of interest here for analysis. While biological individuals get on with breeding that makes relevance for taxonomic categories (species, genera, etc.), and hence are the central level of importance for biology, here in sex work research, it is the categories that are central to our concerns. But again, these are species, genera, families. However, the field analyst's question would be something like: what species of sex work are carried out here in this city/ place/state/country? It is a broad categorical question. It is never intended to be a specific question addressed to individual sex workers.

Back to the theory

Consider prostitution as a phenomenon which moves through a social system or a cultural space in a manner akin to information moving as a set of signals would through a noisy channel. We can follow Shannon who took the original entropy expression and gave it meaning for information theory, as the shortage of information in a message, or missing amounts of information between transmission and reception. Thus information is about uncertainty.

Let $H(y)$ be the entropy of the prostitution output, which is seen as a log function of the sum of the force or strength of prostitution to go on, to drive forward, to evolve z, and the force to oppose or stop prostitution, bring about its abolition, drive it down η. Further, let $H(n)$ represent the entropy of the noise, which is a log function of that opposing force alone.

That is,

$$H(y) = f(Z + \eta) \qquad (2.4)$$

while

$$H(n) = f(\eta) \qquad (2.5)$$

where the functions f are logarithmic.

It follows that the amount of prostitution P, in such a system, akin to channel capacity in information theory (Shannon & Weaver 1998:99), would be given by

$$P = H(y) - H(n).$$

Substituting from the log functions (2.4) and (2.5),

$$P = A \log\left[(Z + \eta)/\eta\right]$$

or as such an expression is more commonly written

$$P = A \log(1 + Z/\eta) \qquad (2.6)$$

where A is the least upper bound of prostitution taxa referred to earlier.

In this form we recognise the Shannon-Hartley theorem, the so-called noisy channel coding theorem, the fundamental theorem of information theory.

Note that in equation (2.6) P is a measure of the amount of prostitution, A is the level of prostitution any given society will tolerate (which for my purposes here is estimated in terms of an upper bound number of species), Z is the strength, drive or energy of prostitution as a social phenomenon, and η is the strength or energy of abolitionist, impeding or removalist forces in that society. That is, social factors seeking to block or stop prostitution.

With built-in caveats about coding or what is called self-checking, Shannon proved – and this is the important part for us - that provided transmission is kept within channel capacity, in a noisy channel, a signal could always be sent virtually without distortion.

Such a conclusion gives to equation (2.6) significant implications. Equation (2.6) appears to hold within itself important explanatory and predictive powers. It brings us to a surprising and unexpected, almost counterintuitive position: no matter how much social noise there is – abolitionist, moral campaigning, eradication programs – prostitution, like entropy, like Shannon's noisy channel signal, will prevail, eventually.

Which is to say prostitution can be seen as an unstoppable phenomenon. In the manner of the second law of thermodynamics and its provision for us of entropy, we can write this as

$$dP \geq 0 \qquad (2.7)$$

where P is a measure of prostitution as above and the differential dP is an infinitesimal change in P. In the most benign case, where nothing is going on, dP is at worst equal to zero. It remains the same. In the normal course of all cultural and social change, dP is greater than zero. That is, prostitution never decreases and is in effect unstoppable. It steamrollers any attempts to abolish it or drive it down through legislation, policing, etc. The facts bear this out, as do the observations of them by others (e.g. Goodall 1996).

In Walters (2013:357) I wrote:

> prostitution will diversify under suitable conditions,
> which appear to be growth in wealth, decline in wealth, re-
> distribution of wealth, and any equivalent of postmodern
> capitalist values relating to lifestyles and consumption
> among young men and women (boys and girls). In fact, the
> data seem to suggest that prostitution will increase given
> virtually any sort of reasonably rapid and widespread
> social change.

This concluded a section where I had drawn the above inference from empirical evidence gained from my own Vietnamese work, as well as examples from sex work literature on Japan, Malaysia and Indonesia. We can now see that such a conclusion is in fact predicted by the above relation (2.7). It is quite satisfying to be able to add to a theory such as this does, finding it in fact predicts something I had already demonstrated empirically in a previous work.

Now, the final term of equation (2.6) may be written as

$$U = Z / \eta$$

where the symbols Z and η are as just given, while U becomes a measure of what I will term the unstoppability of prostitution. For U to ever be zero, Z basically has to be zero. That is, a Very Big Hierarchy society has to suddenly lose its drive for prostitution, something that has never happened in the six to seven thousand years that prostitution has been a part of the planet's social and cultural fabric (see chapter 3). Alternatively, η – effort of forces opposed to prostitution - has to be so great that U is rendered effectively zero, for example 0.0000001, and the bracketed term of equation (2.6) to a four-place decimal sum of one, whereupon all evolution of prostitution stops (because log 1 = 0). Apart from 6,000 or more years of history, the global ethnographic data suggest most strongly that this is highly unlikely. In fact, the data from China in Table 6.1 of Walters (2013), using the number of species S_T as the key variable (S_T standing symbolically for species total), imply that at very worst scenario levels U is likely to minimise at about a quarter or a fifth ($U \sim 0.20 - 0.25$).

John MacArthur adapted the theory (2.6) for rate of evolution in animal biodiversity. However, he said that the key parameters (given as A and Z in the above equation) were without meaning in ecology and had to be determined in each individual context by regression methods. But, one thing that was important – suggested to MacArthur by Robert May - was that the left hand side value for rate of evolution could be equally substituted as S_T, yielding the formula for a logseries distribution of species abundance. My adaptation of the Shannon formula together with this variant from MacArthur, give to the equation, unlike that in ecology, clear cultural and social meanings for all variables. And the log series distribution becomes crucial for the theory.

For the Chinese data from Table 6.1 of Walters (2013) then, with

$$U = Z / \eta$$

and following MacArthur, whereby the equation can be modified as

$$S_T = A \log(1 + U)$$

I showed that the theory could be used to predict the number of species of prostitution expected in Vietnam during the post-1975 communist removal period. (During that period the Vietnamese authorities claimed they had eradicated prostitution, meaning that the number of species observable at that time according to them was zero.)

Let us arbitrarily set the tolerance level for prostitution types A in the earlier and communist historical periods of Vietnam at 30 species, estimated from a likely upper bound given the data in Table 6.1 of Walters (2013). The unstoppability term U can be estimated from Chinese data by the ratio of surviving species under Chinese communist removal against number of taxa in the earlier historical period (all this Chinese information is taken from Hershatter 1997). That number was 7/29 = 0.2413…, which gave a value for S_T, number of species observable in the communist removal period in Vietnam, as 6.45. Plus or minus random errors, let us say 6 species of prostitution. All of these calculations are also set out in Walters (2013).

So the theory is testable. The above prediction is quantitatively assessable by investigative historians of Vietnam under the communists. If they can be urged to undertake research akin to the superb work Hershatter did for Shanghai, testing of the theory becomes possible.

Now, I said earlier that prostitution is unstoppable, unless it isn't. What did I mean by that odd and somewhat contradictory statement? Consider time going into the future, which we'll call t. If there exists a time period m, $1 < m < t$, where prostitution fails to exist, such as in Nazi Germany, Pol Pot Cambodia, or as was purportedly the case for both China and Vietnam under the new communist regimes of the 1950s and 1970s respectively, then as it exists in its origin period, which we'll call $P(1)$, and continues to exist in contemporary times $P(now)$, there must be a time period $m + a$, where a is another natural number 1,2,3…, $1 < (m + a) < t$, such that in that time period prostitution rejuvenates, becomes vigorous again. As it thus exhibits stability or resilience, returning to its equilibrium condition after perturbation, prostitution is again shown to be unstoppable.

Therefore for any n in set N, of time periods, $P(n)$ holds unless, I'll say it again, it doesn't. Which means that unless some external catastrophe occurs either out of the blue or scientifically predicted, terminating life, terminating the universe, etc., prostitution will be with us forever. The only thing that can stop it is our demise as a species before we have had a chance to colonise other parts of the universe, as the Earth is swallowed by the Sun, etc. Failing that, it is unstoppable.

The third law of thermodynamics shows the impossibility of a system attaining Absolute zero temperature. But, and this is a big and important but, with an ever expanding universe expanding at an increasing rate, if, and this is a big if, in billions of year from now, the cold dark almost empty universe does attain such a seemingly impossible temperature, then at that point and that point only, entropy fails to increase and for the first and unique time the universe attains the position

$$dS = 0.$$

It dies. My theory of unstoppable prostitution follows this exactly and metaphorically. Prostitution is unstoppable, unless, like entropy, it isn't. Which is to say, that as long as normal conditions prevail, prostitution will continue forever. No police or courts or abolitionists will be able to stop it, at least in the long haul. Temporarily perhaps, by the deployment of arch fascist methods, but not permanently. However, the universe might. Of course our species will go extinct, eventually. If we have not sent colonists - be they biological or intelligent machines - out to other parts of the galaxy or universe generally when that happens, prostitution like all of our descendants, is doomed. That's the "unless it isn't" clause. I call it the Newtonian caveat.

We can formalize this Newtonian caveat according to a statement of Newton's first law of motion, as:

$$\sum F = 0 \Rightarrow \frac{dv}{dt} = 0$$

where F is force, v is velocity and t is time. These relations tell us: when the sum of forces acting on a body is zero, this implies that there is no change (in this case acceleration given by $dv \ / \ dt$) in motion of the body. To have change, there must be an outside force acting. Thus, unless there is that external force such as the sun engulfing the Earth as it moves down the Hertzsprung-Russell main sequence (see Silk 1980, Adams & Laughlin 1997) and as a red giant engulfs the solar system, or whatever, again, before we have had a chance to colonise the universe, prostitution is set to be unstoppable now and forever more.

Summary & Conclusions

In this chapter I have introduced the theory of unstoppable prostitution. I presented a brief discussion of the major natural unstoppable phenomenon, entropy. This idea is developed by taking a lead from the second law of thermodynamics, especially the notion that in the course of spontaneous change, the entropy of the universe increases. This was then linked with the interpretation of entropy as uncertainty or diversity. In turn these were shown to be integrally related to information theory. From the fundamental work on this last set of ideas, due to Claude Shannon, I derived the theory.

It says: prostitution will continue forever, unable to be stopped by social, cultural or political forces, at least in the long haul. With one caveat: it can of course be stopped by such natural phenomena as biological extinction or cosmological catastrophe. For then, all babies go out with the bathwater.

The theory is a surprising and unexpected outcome of introducing a species concept into sex work research. Reference to bar girls, call girls, or temporary wives as particular species of prostitution or sex work allows the use of the most simple measure of ecological diversity: the total number of species S_T. So any jurisdiction in any given historical period can be characterised by the number of species of prostitution present in the society or some given social setting. This not only permitted development of the quantitative picture necessary for the theory, but also allows the theory to be tested empirically by future investigative historians.

In Walters (2013) I stressed that amid all the bright lights and glamour of theory, the implications are nevertheless extremely grounded and pragmatic. They are principally that prostitution can continue as an industry content in the belief that despite the best efforts of gainsaying authorities, their livelihood potential will continue. I do so stress again here. The pleasant and positive outcomes of the theory are to make it clear that do-gooder abolitionists may as well give up and turn their energies and attention to some more useful and positive activities. For in the long haul they will never defeat prostitution.

I hope sex workers and their support staff are able to see this as much more than academic wank. The power of this theory, for all its arcane and esoteric nuances, is that it gives to us a political confidence never before attained logically and deductively, except in hope and perhaps insightful opinion: that your work can and will continue forever. Yes it will change over time. Yes it will adapt. But no amount of abolitionist activity, lobby group pressure, legislative changes, periods of policing enthusiasm, will stop it. Stand in its way they will, continue to arrest and prosecute they will; make a nuisance of themselves for hard working people they will. But the political fight must be taken up to do-gooders and self-designed puritans on that account. Notice that confidence can accrue from this theory: that the do-gooders have no chance; they will not win. Cannot win. Prostitution will be the winner, and in a civilised world of the future, will prevail to the end.

One highly desirable corollary of this is as follows: if the theory is recognised and accepted in civilised societies of the future, social power can be handed to sex workers universally. Then the industry, organised into unions or professional associations, with standard accoutrements of civilised industries such as continuing education, health clinics, child care facilities, etc., for workers, can finally be free of the cheap tawdry organised crime that benefits now and has in the past, from the context prostitution is thrust into by do-gooders: of a pariah industry operating at the edges of respectability falling victim to the unruly and corrupt who would prey upon it and its practitioners.

CHAPTER 3

Recent Prostitution

So, prostitution is unstoppable. In this chapter, to continue the metaphor of the Introduction, I examine the function that is prostitution over time from the other end: namely, its beginning. Consideration of available historical and ethnographic evidence leads to the suggestion that this beginning is recent. Prostitution has only been with us for a relatively short while.

The term Recent in the title has an intended double meaning. I argue, following the absence of evidence for prostitution for the bulk of human history, for it to have only been around in recent millennia: the 7,000 years or so before present in which we have had cities and states as social forms in human life. That is, during the existence of what I am calling Very Big Hierarchy (VBH) societies, most commonly referred to in the literature as complex societies. These societies have only been in existence for one thousandth of human history. As I said in chapter 1, I will argue that it is civilization that gives us prostitution. Recent phenomena, these.

To get the second meaning we need to recognise that this last geological period, the one in which we now live, is known as the Holocene. It is the time since the end of the last Pleistocene Ice Age. The Pleistocene to Holocene transition can be seen as beginning some 10,000 or so years ago. In historical geology and Earth history, the Holocene period is alternatively termed the Recent. Prostitution appears to be a Recent phenomenon.

I look at the extensive historical archaeological and ethnographic record in search of prostitution. For most of human existence there is none to be found. Humans and our immediate ancestors, the various species of hominids (Family Hominidae), have walked the planet for some 6 million years. For 99.999% of that time these creatures lived as hunters and gatherers, mostly in small social groups, foraging plant and animal foods across the space of their territories. (Of course, some indigenous peoples continue to forage today, as least as part of their economic round.) As far as I am aware, no archaeologist of any hunting species, from the first Australopithecines of the African savannah through to our modern global human ancestors or contemporaries, has ever uncovered interpretable remains of evidence for endogenous prostitution occurring in their societies. Likewise researchers of recent history as well as ethnographers who travelled the globe in the footsteps of imperialist colonialism to work among native peoples, have not been known to mention prostitution occurring in those cultures. In the third section of the chapter I largely repeat this empirical claim, at slightly more length.

That section presents evidence but also has to deal with the issue of absence of evidence. While is it fairly easy to present an absence of evidence for the existence of prostitution for the greater part of human history, translating that absence of evidence into evidence of absence is potentially rather more tricky. Some faith is perhaps required. Well, argument by analogy, inference or induction is at least needed. To this end I open the discussion with a slight digression which provides relevant analogy and inference from that part of cosmology and astronomy dealing with the search for extra terrestrial intelligence (SETI). I will argue, as the cosmologists have indeed done for the absence of extra terrestrial intelligent life, that the absence of evidence for pre-VBH prostitution constitutes the reality: evidence for absence.

Following the discussion of there being no evidence for prostitution in data from the past, the chapter then gives a sketch of the kinds of societies found on the planet prior to or extra to, VBH societies. Following the great anthropologist Marshall Sahlins (1974), I label these as societies with a Domestic Mode of Production (DMP societies). These are the hunting and gathering cultures as well as hunting horticulturalists, farmers and agriculturalists of the post-Pleistocene era. For these last still organised their cultures and economies, as well shall see, according to what we might term DMP principles.

Then in the Recent the breakout occurs that gives us VBH societies: cities, states, city-states, empires, and the attributes that accompany such social forms: kings, generals, accountants, priests, bureaucrats, proletariats, warfare, large irrigation schemes, agricultural and market economies, taxes, poverty, prostitution.

When the transition happens to VBH societies in certain parts of the world, I argue that the results, the above listed attributes, can be viewed as what I call the VBH set. This is a set with new and unique attributes for human history. To put this in perspective, I introduce a very short excursion into set theory. This shows it to be a useful and appropriate theoretical structure with which to begin this consideration of the social transitions that occurred in these places at these times.

Then follow several sections of fairly serious theory. I have argued since the opening sentences of the book that prostitution can be seen as a function of some other variable which changes over time. (For simplicity's sake I will only consider a single causal variable, leaving aside the perhaps more realistic but mathematically less tractable multi-variable possibility.) Consideration of such a function that represents some feature of history leads us into more mathematical entanglements. For such a function can be represented by what mathematicians call a power series. This entails a certain representation of a function by expanding it about a centre. This may all seem terribly convoluted. However, we gain richly from this apparent digression into convolution. For it emerges that such a power series allows us to account for the historical distribution of prostitution over time (for most of the time not there, then suddenly there and everywhere), as well as make some predictions which can be tested.

If we choose our power series appropriately, we find it provides for us a beginning for prostitution in the manner suggested by the empirical absence of evidence over history. Such an approach may seem like an overstatement of a simple problem using unnecessarily mathematical window dressing. However, the approach chosen fits the data and locates nicely the switchover from the proposed absence of prostitution to its presence. So the big advantage of this rather technical stuff is that it fits exactly with what an empirical pattern of absence, followed by presence, should look like. Hence it allows us to strengthen our claims that the absence of evidence for prostitution is actually matched, via theory, to evidence for absence.

This all entails a discussion of hierarchy, as I noted in the Introduction (chapter 1). I derive that variable here then offer an index for its measurement. Finally for the maths, I provide a very simple numerical example to show how such a hierarchy index would work to describe changes from DMP to VBH societies.

At the end of the chapter I ask if we can determine when prostitution began? I return to history and contemporary accounts of prostitution from writers such as Herodotus and ancient anonymous scribes. I also ask archaeologists of VBH societies to return to their data and see if they can operationalise variables that may assist in the search for early prostitution (e.g. bedrooms of similar or dormitory size and structure, sleeping platforms, artefacts excavated therein, etc.).

Following the argument above, the VBH set is seen to contain prostitution as an element. My final brush up with mathematics is not calculation per se, but more a plea to mathematicians to develop some tools and techniques that may help here. Just as I ask archaeologists to come up with key empirical variables, the theory would be greatly advanced if mathematicians could create for us a kind of set-element relation of the following kind. I suggest it is helpful to introduce a new kind of set, called here obligate sets. This would provide a category for the kind of set I am thinking about when I talk of the VBH set.

If there is a price to be paid for the introduction in this chapter of a cascade of mathematical clutter, culminating in a plea for new sets, we also become conscious of a reward. The gains we make are in the glimpses of gravity given to a cluster of ideas for which there is currently only the scantiest of historical and archaeological evidence. Potentially testable predictions bob up all through the chapter. These are found to fit nicely with the history of culture and society as we know it. Also, we can, with tolerance for leaps of faith, find a prediction at the end that may set archaeologists off (once they've stopped snickering) searching through their field data for a beginning to Recent prostitution.

Fermi's dilemma

The Nobel Prize winning physicist Enrico Fermi who, among other things, achieved the first nuclear chain reaction, addressed the possibility of there being intelligent extra terrestrial life. He asked the following question: if they're out there, why haven't we heard from them? This encapsulates what we might call Fermi's dilemma. It has become known in the literature, incorrectly, as Fermi's paradox – e.g. Circovic 2005, 2008. But it is not a paradox at all. It is what's called an if-then conditional (Priest 2000:47). (Remember that a paradox takes the simple form, for example: *this statement is false*. By being true, the statement is immediately false; but conversely, by being false it becomes immediately true. That's a paradox.)

If there is extra terrestrial intelligent life, especially if it is highly so, more so than us, say, *then* their capacity for telecommunications, rocketry, space travel, computing, etc., should de sufficiently advanced for there to have been some successful attempts made to contact other intelligent life, i.e. we Earthlings for example.

There has been much debate over this issue. One of the consequences of this has been the money and effort put into Search for Extra Terrestrial Intelligence (SETI) programs of various sorts over the decades. But still we fail to find them. Hence I will briefly sketch here an outline of the argument, following from this result, that there is no Extra Terrestrial Intelligent life (ETI). Since they are not here, this implies they do not exist (Barrow & Tipler 1986:576). Its relevance as analogy will become clear: a similar line of reasoning may be applied to conclude that prior to VBH societies, there was no prostitution.

Barrow & Tipler (1986:577-581) argue that with such telecommunications (including radio transmission of course), computing, and rocketry skills, such an intelligent form of life should be able to explore the galaxy in less than 300 million years. In fact, with such technology they calculate that transit time to the nearest stars should only be about 10^4 or 10^5 years – a long time yes, but quite short compared with stellar and planetary lifetimes since their beginning, which are usually measured in billions of years. Our evolution to technological ability to communicate thus, occurred within 5 billion years of the formation of our planet. It should follow that other technologically similar species could be expected to evolve in at least that time. So were they especially near us, they have had plenty of time for contact.

On that account, and as a result of all the fruitless searching we have done, "one fact stands out at the present time: there is no evidence whatsoever of intelligent life having any significant effect upon the Universe in the large" (Barrow & Tipler 1986: 613). "It is important to note" caution Barrow & Tipler (1986:590), that the above conclusion depends on the "*observed evidential* fact" (emphasis in original) that ETI is not present in our solar system. This is not a situation of absence of evidence. There is evidence that ETI are absent. Then from this observed fact, it can be inferred as a logical consequence that ETI are absent from our galaxy (Barrow & Tipler 1986:590). And further, as they say above, from the universe in the large.

Prostitution in the historical & ethnographic record

No ethnographic records exist for prostitution occurring in DMP societies of the type traditionally studied by anthropologists through the nineteenth, twentieth and twenty-first centuries. Of course, once global mercantile capitalism and its companion traveller, proselytising christianity, spread into all corners of the world, prostitution followed as sure as did introduced diseases, germs, guns and the One True Redeemer (see Diamond 1999). But during times when DMP societies were not yet alienated by the effects of state borders, modern towns and cities, colonial control, legislation and policing, there is no evidence for anything we could begin to label as prostitution.

One important corollary of this is that talk of prostitution being "always" with us as "the oldest profession" is so far wide of the mark as regards what has actually transpired in human history (Walters 2013), that such claims reek of clichéd nonsense. Such statements, devoid of fact as they are, belong in the same basket as the origin myths promulgated by those who believe that certain texts retain veracity when suggesting the world is of the order of a few thousand years old, and we humans along with it emerging from a past of that length. (In such fantasies we have always lived in cities and had prostitutes.)

The DMP societies recorded by contemporary and historical ethnographers knew no such phenomenon. We can follow the reasoning in the inference drawn by Barrow & Tipler (1986:590) above to conclude: from the observed fact that there was no prostitution in DMP societies recorded by anthropologists and historians, we can draw the logical consequence that prior to the onset of VBH societies, prostitution was unknown.

This allows us to also infer that all previous societies known to us only from archaeology, which were of the same order of population size, which pursued similar economic practices, which operated through similar levels of hierarchy, that they too were totally unfamiliar with prostitution. Critics might think this a large leap of faith. But it isn't. If we put in place a set of attributes of all recorded DMP societies in regards to size, territorial and social organisation, rank and hierarchy, lack of money and material culture as we know them in the modern world, economy, and belief systems, it becomes an obvious and valid inference to conclude that all DMP societies that ever existed had no other additional set of system properties from which to organise their own particular and often unique cultures and societies. Therefore recorded DMP societies without prostitution lead, I suggest, to a valid inference that societies described by archaeology and ancient history as possessing this same suite of key cultural elements, were also devoid of prostitution.

The human lineage has occupied a place on the planet for some 6 million years. Known taxonomically as the Family Hominidae, this family of man, or family of humans, separated off from some primate ancestor we shared with creatures who became the modern great apes, 6 million years ago give or take. Those initial ancestors, small creatures about the size of a modern chimpanzee, known collectively as the Australopithecines, moved with changing climates and environmental conditions, out of the forests of sub-Saharan Africa onto the savannah where they were able to leave their evolutionary legacy.

We don't know very much about their social organisation and cultural capacities. But we do know these things: two primate forms successfully colonised the savannah at this time; one of which became the quadrupedal baboons we are familiar with today; the other, a forest brachiator with longish forelimbs and hands capable of clutching, became out ancestor (Foley 1995). Somewhere in there – the data are not exactly clear as to when – with vertebral column, pelvis, knee, and foot bones all adjusted over time by evolutionary changes, this lineage of ours stood upright and walked bipedally in much the same way we as hominids have done ever since.

As the first identified hominid bones occur in the fossil record around 6 million years ago, so by 4 million years before present, we can be sure – from radiometric dating of rocks and fossils – that these ancestors were walking (and in groups too, take note) upright and in bipedal fashion we are all familiar with today. A group of them, whose footprints were left in mud beside a lake at a place called Laetoli in east Africa, then soon after covered for the aeons by a shower of volcanic dust, suggest a family on a stroll with, at one moment, a small individual stepping in the footprints made by the adult it was following. A child at play!

That's a big call on social organisation. Stronger evidence comes from the history of social organisation shown by most of the largeish primates, creatures similar to those who tossed up the DNA for our lineage founders. It is this: they lived in groups, many of which pass any anthropologist's definition of families. The group stays together for hunting, gathering, feeding, sharing, child care, female protection, and so on. Human social organisation was not invented in the most recent few thousand years and recorded immediately by the scribes of some particular belief system hermetically ready for Rousseau, Hobbes and Locke to lay claim to. It has been with us in this form from early primate days. We did not become human and garner our modern social organisation from moonshine and lightning strikes, or any other mumbo-jumbo such as decisions by sapient individuals to abandon the state of nature and establish a social contract. We crossed our ancestral lineage boundaries, in those early forest days, with maybe some modifications made on the savannah, as primates. That is, as social creatures. When we became human we were already social. We were animals who live in and act out lives as, families.

We don't need me to get carried away any further. I will simply make the underlying point. Comparative evolutionary studies show our lineage organised in groups, many definable as families, from the outset. Archaeology shows us small groups, hunting and gathering, feeding, sharing, fighting, contesting, and later, after about 2.5 million years ago, stone tool using. Not one shred of this comparative or archaeological evidence suggests anything like the kind of material wealth, hierarchy and social organisation required for prostitution.

Some time after stone tools enter the record, about 2 million years ago, our ancestors, or some of them, upped and left Africa. Creatures similar to the standard text book species *Homo erectus* (formerly known by such popular but inaccurate names as Peking Man and Java Man) colonised to the north and east, southwestern Asia, Europe, the subcontinental area, eastern Europe, east Asia and Southeast Asia as far as present-day Java, which then was a string of high mountains and plateau adjacent the coast of the ancient continent we now call Sundaland.

Then by sometime around or just before 100,000 years ago, two large brained hominids evolve: *Homo neanderthalensis* (the Neandertals) and *Homo sapiens* (we, us, modern humans). The former first appear in the record in southwestern Asia while the latter appear to have evolved in southern Africa, whence they too, like their erectine forbears, send a contingent on a move out of Africa to take over the world.

It is this latter species, our own species, that alone would emerge from the Ice Age as the planet's sole hominid survivor taxon. It is our species, modern humans, who would be in the right – if that's a proper term – place at the appropriate time, to take advantage of climate change, plants expanding their distribution and abundance, especially seed grasses flourishing, and various other conditions which made it suitable to begin to think about utilising all this as a means to living in different sorts of cultures, societies and then economies. They took up agriculture as the post-Ice conditions proved suitable for such food-getting practices. But these agricultural societies, like their descendants who have been with us until recently in parts of Africa, Melanesia, North & South America, and parts of Asia, took as their social forms the DMP.

And when do the constellations align for all this to happen? At the onset of the Holocene. Initially in southwestern Asia. Then elsewhere. But further changes were in store.

We witness the onset of what most archaeologists now refer to as complex societies, and for which I am introducing the term VBH societies. In the Holocene or Recent period. Some 7000 or 6000 years before present. Which is to say, given we have walked the earth for 6 million years, one thousandth of the time we have existed as socially organised hominids. For 999 thousandths of that time, hominid and human social organisation remained uncontaminated by prostitution.

There are documentary records of prostitution in places like Babylon and Egypt some 3000 years ago (Herodotus 1988:80, 121-122, 177, 179, 182, etc.). Then of course, every VBH society thereafter has its prostitution. So we have a data dilemma here. For 99.999% of hominid evolution, we gain glimpses of societies without prostitution. Then we have a gap in the record, where VBH societies are developing and asserting their presence. However, for the first 4000 or so years of VBH social organisation there are no records of prostitution. But this is mainly due to the lack of records full stop. We have to wait for the discovery of writing which, coincidentally, also flourishes some 3000 years or so after the first VBH societies arrive. Then from about 3000 years before present there it is, prostitution recorded, talked about, taken for granted, on tablets, on stone, on parchments.

What does this mean? On the one hand it may imply that VBH societies got going without prostitution, which came on the social scene some 4000 years later. On the other hand it may be that prostitution came into being as the other key elements of VBH social organisation did, but remained archaeologically invisible for 4000 years until we begin to unearth written records. How do we test this? I'm not sure, but I will make a few tentative suggestions at the end of the chapter.

Before we go there though, there are some housekeeping things we need to take care of. It is time to say some more about both DMP and VBH societies in general.

DMP societies

The Domestic Mode of Production (DMP) is a concept we owe to Marshall Sahlins (1974). Most of what follows in this section is taken from Sahlins' summaries, analysis, and argument. The page numbered quotes refer to the relevant *Stone Age Economics* chapters on the DMP.

DMP societies are the hunters, gatherers, pastoralists and horticulturalists who lived in small scale societies with minimal ranking or hierarchy, basing their social life on kinship and domestic production. They are the indigenous hunters of the Arctic, of Australia, South Africa and North America, the swidden agriculturalists of tropical South America, tropical Southeast Asia, of Melanesia, the hunter-horticulturalists of the Pacific, the pastoralists of northeast Africa. They are peoples with names made famous by ethnography: the Eskimo, the Trobriand Islanders, the Nuer, the Andaman Islanders, the Tikopia, Maori, Hawaiians, Fijians, Samoans, the !Kung, the Yanomamo, the Huron, the Mohawk, the Nootka, the Bella Coola, the Kwakiutl, Cherokee and Sioux, the Aranda, Yir Yiront, and Tiwi.

These are peoples who prior to invasions into their lifestyle by christian colonialists and capitalists, lived without states, without cities, without armies, without police forces, without taxes, and largely without money economies. Even though many of these groups are extant, and live now within the boundaries of modern states, articulating with global capitalism, I am concerned, as was Sahlins, with their pre-capitalist social forms. Hence even though I use present tense in the section, I am well aware the past tense would perhaps be more appropriate as a means of evoking what anthropologists like to call traditional lifestyles.

These peoples live with economies organised according to kinship relations and domestic groups, where underproduction is the norm. Resources are typically under used, labour power is under used. A customary working day is often short, often interrupted, separated by days of slack, as well as sleep, ceremony and visiting. Sometimes there is seasonal variation in production, and people are typically under employed.

The DMP is characterised by being an economy of production for use, for the livelihood of the producers. As production is instituted by domestic groups, usually constituted as families of one kind or another, it is geared to customary requirements. Production is for the benefit of the producers.

People are malleable, as well as important. Social and political pressures come up with the most feasible strategy. Production is for use value, for livelihood, and not for profit. No compulsion to surplus output is built into the DMP. The system defines its own sufficiency, and thence does not realise the surplus of which it is perfectly capable. In DMP societies, economics is only a part-time activity, or at least an activity of only part of the society. In other words, the economy is a function of society. It is yet another cultural phenomenon or cultural dimension.

Everything is organised by and around domestic groups. Yet a fair percentage of domestic groups fail to produce their own livelihood, even though they are organised to do so. There is large variation in household production, including these cases of failure. Production differences are normally distributed, and "insofar as [production] is organised by domestic groups, it is established on a fragile and vulnerable base" (p.74).

The DMP is truly a society without a sovereign. The "social economy is fragmented into a thousand petty existences, each organized to proceed independently of the others and each dedicated to the homebred principle of looking out for itself" (p.95). It is a paradigm of anarchy.

Yet of course existence is ordered and, as in all cultures, people obey rules, are socialised into beliefs about the good life and moral behaviour. There are strict rules and taboos, with kinship and religion governing the protocols and rituals of both daily life and ceremonial performance. Mostly people live in dispersed hamlets and villages, if they are settled horticulturalists say, or in temporary camps set up for fishing, hunting, fruiting seasons, or ceremony if they are mobile hunters and gatherers. But even these latter move about only on their own territory, where boundaries, though not drawn on maps or marked by military outposts, are strictly observed. (These break down at times of friendly entrances for shared ceremony or unfriendly ones for raids on cattle or enemies.)

Hierarchy is limited in the DMP. There are universal observances according to sex and age. Females usually defer in contexts of public face and performance at least, to their males, father, elder brother, husband, eldest son even. However, there are lots of recorded situations where women remain a (clichéd) power behind the throne, as it were. Or, to avoid that cliché, at least serious contributors to a more democratic decision making process. I have seen many an instance both in indigenous Australia and in Southeast Asia where a decision making gathering of men will be offset by lone drifts over to the women's camp or to the females gossiping in the kitchen, to gather opinion, advice, and feelings.

Many a powerful woman can govern by personality and wisdom without ever entering a public forum.

Again, usually, the young defer to the old. Old men and women are vast storehouses of wisdom, kinship knowledge, oral history, and are sought out for advice on same. Senior men may be the best hunters, senior women the most skilled gatherers. Sons will do fathers' bidding, as will daughters be obedient to their mothers. But again, these formalities can break down by the sheer bonds of familial love and duty of care. I have seen a spoilt indulged 10 year old alter the entire next few days' plan of an extended family group simply by throwing a prolonged tantrum to get what it was he desired. That's not democracy. It is, as Sahlins says, a form of paradigmatic anarchy. The only role played by age hierarchy in that particular case, was placation.

My insights, and those of Sahlins, derive from a little more than a hundred years of ethnography. However, an archaeological record of both Recent and Pleistocene hunters gives us the same patterns of small group organisation, dispersed camps, boundaries, hunting, and at the very terminal time of the Ice Age, the beginnings of horticulture. I think we can have confidence that the intersection between archaeological data and the patterns of behaviour observed by anthropologists, give us a DMP lifestyle dating back through most of human existence. There is certainly no hint of anything like Very Big Hierarchy or the prostitution I am seeking in this book.

VBH societies

Then suddenly VBH societies are upon us. Initially in southwestern Asia, then elsewhere in Egypt, in the Indus, in China, and in both Meso and South America. But even then they don't become universal. They exist in tandem with continuing DMP societies, cheek by jowl in some cases as core relates to periphery. In other cases sufficiently separated by mountain or water barriers, they exist oblivious of each other. Then of course, finally, the modern global world we populate is VBH societies all the way down, even if some of these encapsulate cultures which still live out progressive forms of a DMP existence. These latter are inextricably tangled up with markets and government services of the larger VBH state within whose boundaries they live.

VBH societies are marked by attributes such as kings, courts, armies, cities and large towns, bureaucracy, money, writing, monumental architecture, and state based or national religions. It is my argument in this chapter that prostitution comes into existence as well at this time, as yet one more key element of VBH societies.

The empirical evidence of the history of social hierarchy shows the function describing that history to be discontinuous with almost no growth over the nearly 6 million years of the Pliocene and Pleistocene. For all that while it appears hominids were practising a DMP lifestyle. A little more hierarchy came into being in occasional DMP societies such as those on the Northwest Coast (NWC) of North America, as well as in the early agricultural societies from Southwest Asia at the terminal Pleistocene. Then suddenly there is this dramatic discontinuity. I will have more to say about this below, and in chapter 4. But first, some theory.

Theory tells us that the set of all points (elements) of such a discontinuity may be what is termed a discrete set, or it can be one of certain other kinds of sets. In accord with being a discrete set, it has elements which are both isolated and countable (see below). Set theory can thus be seen to provide a useful and productive metaphor for describing the new and discontinuous elements which characterise the onset of VBH societies.

I refer to this list of unique new cultural, social and political attributes as the VBH set, and describe it in more detail in the following section.

Set theory

Set theory can be deployed to help with some insights into the issues concerning the onset of Very Big Hierarchy and VBH societies. It allows us to see properties of social structure as elements of sets, thereby separating out and bringing clearly into relief those particular attributes that define VBH societies.

If an object o is a member of a set A, we write $o \in A$. A number of axioms and operations define sets. For example, sets exist in a universe, with the complement of a set being all that exists in that universe outside the set. Sets are made up of members or elements, which themselves may be sets. A set may have no elements, then referred to as an empty set. Sets can overlap, their joint sections being called an intersection. They can be added together under an operation called union. If an element is in a set A, and A is itself a member of set B, then that element is also a member of B. And so on.

A universe, or class, contains as elements all the entities one wishes to consider in a given situation. So to consider social structure one might want to include all the relevant attributes that define such an entity. For example, family, social roles, economic roles, religion, material culture, and so on. Such a universe can be referred to as a von Neumann universe V, or alternatively it is known as a constructible universe, as L, where the fundamental axiom of constructibility is $V = L$. V is the set of all the subsets that have gone before, or make up the set. For example for any set $\{x,y,z\}$, then $V = \{0, x, y, z, xy, xz, yz, xyz\}$.

The advantage of working with a constructible universe is that we do not have to include all prior sets as members, but can select the elements we want from their defined state, certain parameters they may have, etc. This means we do not have to add every element that has ever been part of hominid societies to the set of attributes of VBH societies. For example as above, we can define our members as having neither an empty set nor any x. The constructible class is then L = {y,z,yz}. This is realistic and characterises social history nicely, as attributes of social structure drop out of use or relevance over time, often as a result of being replaced by new forms.

We best begin thinking through hominid history however, utilising the von Neumann universe. This is a cumulative hierarchy, which is in turn a collection of sets V_α where α is an ordinal number, such that

V_0 = the empty set,

for any β, $V_{\beta+1}$ is the power set M of V_β,

and, for any limit ordinal λ, $V_\lambda := U_{\beta<\lambda} V_\beta$.

This in turn means that $V_\alpha := U_{\beta<\lambda} V_{\beta+1,}$

which immediately brings quite a useful conclusion for our theory. It means that over the long haul of generalised hominid history, which is the universe of our interest in this particular situation, the cumulative hierarchy of attributes, also known as the von Neumann universe, is the union of all subsets of attributes that have gone before, and make up the so-called power set M of V_β.

Which is to say, the hominid past is cumulative. While of course each particular culture came and went, some passing, some showing longer duration continuity, all the while expressing such difference as shown in recent times between central Australian bands, Inuit canoeists from Greenland to northern Canada, and Northwest Coast Pacific salmon hunters. These varied cultures were free to pick and choose their own attributes, making them as vastly diverse as the three cultural clusters just mentioned. Nevertheless, what the theory suggests, and what remains empirically true, is that the general picture of nearly six million years of hunting and gathering is a tapestry of cumulative cultural pattern.

For example, there is a time before 2.4 million years before present, when no stone artefacts were made or used by our hominid ancestors. From that time on, stone is present in global hominid material culture, among all forms of human ancestors and modern humans as well.

Concerning this, two more key features emerge from the theory. One is that there is a cumulative sequence of developments that characterise hominid history. This is not to relapse into the unsupported stage ideas of nineteenth century cultural evolutionists, nor to embrace the twentieth century apologia to this from Leslie White. For any good sense that can be taken from their theories (and there is some, see chapter 4), is militated against by weak flaccid woolly undefined ideas of cultural development, progress or advancement. But on the other hand, it is to suggest, with the support of the empirical evidence of history, that cultural traits are added to social structures cumulatively. Time before stone, time after stone. The metaphor for additive cultural innovation is a curve which is concave up; which is to say a curve growing somewhat like bank interest. It is possessed of an arrow, every bit as clear and strong as that of entropy and the arrow of time. In fact, to pursue the metaphor, it could be argued that cultural entropy always increases with time.

But note most carefully: this, unlike nineteenth century social evolution, is not value added. There is no implication of progress or development or advancement associated with some property we might call goodness or betterment. Nor does it mean, as the nineteenth century theorists argued, that each and every culture passes along the same linear path. In fact here I am not talking about each and every culture, but rather the broad sweep of global culture. It is simply aligning history and theory: things change over time, with a general human cumulative accretion of cultural traits.

The second feature is that there is no going back. As with a cumulative collection of additive sets, addition of culture traits in general does not change direction, there is no reversion. Where a cultural trait is withdrawn from a social structure, where there is a subtraction, an abandonment, equivalence holds good, such that there is no structural reversion. For example, abandoning their king, and the whole concept of a country needing a king, the modern United States of America was founded on what were judged to be more democratic principles. Yet the USA retains an office, the President, as powerful as any king who ever sat on one of history's thrones. Yet the kingly office is now about broader power and wealth sharing. For that same President usually lacks the wealth and hence particular influences of say, top business earners. Power has also come to be shared with the parliament (Congress), the judiciary and occasionally other institutions. Thus it is debateable whether the Presidency is equivalent to a king. For the purposes of the present theory, the Presidency is removed from the set of kings, for while it retains most of the former attributes of status and power, it foregoes some like hereditary and divine rights as well as others like centrally accrued taxes, and centralised personal wealth.

Also, where particular cultural features are lost or abandoned, like the demise of the Australian Democrats political party, or fishing among the ancient Tasmanians, this does not imply reversion. There remains a set which might be called minor political parties. The historical Tasmanians still possessed a set of what might be termed hunting targets – they did not choose starvation or misery by making such a cultural choice.

This feature of the theory predicts the absence in hominid history of any possible reversion such as utopian anarchy (as opposed to DMP anarchy). It renders it no more than a fantasy. For that kind of reversion, from the world we have known for aeons as VBH societies, cannot happen. There will not be an abandonment of government, of the law, of the kinds of hierarchically collective action that leads to armies, cities, and the like. Mind you, if it ever does happen, my theory is rejected. Or at least this aspect of the theory.

However, the theory tells us more. As I said above, VBH societies mark a discontinuity in human history. Various commentators have called that which comes about, a new kind of culture, one that is unique, altering the whole human situation. Toynbee described it as "the emergence of a new species of culture." The theory fits with these empirical observations. Because it describes a constructible universe, one that involves cumulative hierarchy, we see over the long haul of time sets being added in ordinal rank. Then when we get to VBH societies we see the addition of what I now refer to throughout as the VBH set. This is the set of sets that define VBH societies as a completely new phenomenon on planet Earth. Never before in the history of our world or the evolution of life on it has such a happening occurred. It is certainly a unique event, and most certainly an unparalleled cultural construction. The VBH set contains elements of the kind: {king, court, bureaucracy, army, class, appropriated surplus, writing, numeracy, …} never witnessed or recorded before.

So the theory tells us (trivially) that pre-VBH societies have none of these VBH attributes. They are new additions. However, there is far more to this claim than the mere trivial. It means for instance, that in the broad sweep of nearly six million years of hominid history, if ever, and if so wherever and whenever, such attributes threatened to arise singly or in a multi-element set, they were quickly repudiated, rejected, killed off (perhaps literally) before they had a chance to take root. They may of course have been diverted into something culturally and politically acceptable. For example, modern societies record for us historically both the Potlatch Chief among the Northwest Pacific Coast Indians, and the Big Man of Melanesia.

It is possible, and it would fit with the theory, that the incipient beginnings of these institutions had the potential makings of kingship were a suite of other social, cultural, economic and political attributes congruent. They were not. Hence the early invaders and colonisers of these societies recorded institutions which took the forms they did. That is, a central political node (the Potlatch Chief, the Big Man) who appropriated material wealth. But then, unlike the full-blown kings of VBH societies, these figures returned said appropriations to the people via the potlatch and the pig feast. They thereby gained status, but not material wealth. The big breakaway in VBH kingship is wealth appropriated thence retained. How did this happen? I will return to this later (in chapter 4). But first some more theory on the construction of the VBH set.

According to my chosen von Neumann universe V, or the constructible version of it, L, the ordinality of relevant sets would look something like this:

V_0 = the empty set, $\{\}$

which is the set containing zero elements of VBH attributes. In other words it provides for the existence of pre-VBH (DMP) societies in the theory.

$$V_1 = \{\{\}\}$$

the set containing the empty set as an element. This is demanded by the von Neumann theory. It is also the set of all societies that have gone before, each of them devoid of the key VBH elements. It is useful as a reminder that no key institutions from pre-VBH societies remain viable in the new social structure.

$$V_2 = \{\{\{\}\}, \text{surplus}\}$$

the ordinal rank 2 set which adds one element, a surplus, to V_1.

$$V_3 = \{V_2, \text{king}\},$$

$$V_4 = \{V_3, \text{court}\}.$$

The king plus the court he has established around him, together with the economic surplus he has been able to appropriate, bring us to V_4. Remember that these are subsets in their own right with court for example containing elements that look something like

$$C_1 = \{\text{political adviser, finance adviser, military chief, ...}\}.$$

And so it goes, with priests, army, class structure, and many other key attributes such as inventions (writing, mathematics...) being added as the cumulative hierarchy grows and becomes more complex.

These institutions quickly evolve, such that one set (called here R_1) becomes king, his wives (including queen), concubines, princes and princesses. Court advisers become ministers, treasurers, generals, lawyers, surveyors, accountants, etc.

$$R_1 = \{\text{king, queen, prince, princess, duke, count,...}\}$$

while C_1 becomes C_2:

C_2 = {treasurer, finance minister, general, attorney general, high priest,...}.

Until we get a social structure looking something like

V_α = {king, court, army, bureaucracy, cities, state, classes, writing, ...}.

Such is the essential characterisation of this unique new phenomenon called VBH society. V_α is what I referred to above as the VBH set. I merely note in passing that the entire structure hinges on a) the rise of what will hereafter be referred to as the Rogue Individual (RI), and b) his ability to cement his role, convince followers to become his court, his allies, and his muscle power. It is obvious that he must be a good fighter, but most of all a highly skilled politician. He is able to harness this following, then turn it to his desired ends, namely appropriating and retaining surplus, funding an army and being able to exercise total control over it, turning the courtiers to his desired tasks, defining land, measuring, allocating, fencing, appropriating its produce, calculating, taxing, writing laws and statutes that define what he is doing as legal and right, bringing a priestly class into being, convincing them he is the one to be supported in this divine and heavenly quest, and that morality resides in and with him. Then all such allies set about convincing, proselytising or intimidating the masses, who in the new class structure become artisans, workers, vassals and even slaves. They are also required to be the new believers, the worshippers, the followers, the good citizens. I return to this in more theoretical detail in chapter 4.

For while all this is going on, another new element appears in society, and therefore in the VBH set, one never experienced in human history before:

V_σ = {prostitution}.

It too is a set of subsets, one that quickly grows into something like

P = {sex workers, minders, pimps, go-betweens, ...}

all part and parcel of the VBH set.

History as power series

I will return to sets later in the chapter, but first I have to talk a little about history. Let us imagine some historical variable of interest which we will call z. As we would expect for history, z is changing over time. Further, let us imagine a variable of interest which depends on z and changes in accord with it, which we will call $f(z)$. That is, some function of z. Because that's what this book and the theory are about, this latter variable we will call prostitution. I will not define z at this stage, but will return to it later on in the chapter. We can write the functional relationship between the two like this:

z_0	z_1	z_2	z_3	...	z_n
$f(z_0)$	$f(z_1)$	$f(z_2)$	$f(z_3)$	...	$f(z_n)$

Which is to say when $z = z_0$, $f(z) = f(z_0)$, etc. But we still don't really have a feel for $f(z)$. To gain some clearer picture of what the function might look like let us expand it as a power series of the form

$$\sum a_n (z-c)^n \tag{3.1}$$

where c is a constant about which the series is centered and a_n are complex coefficients $a_0, a_1, a_2 ... a_n$. Power series are often centered about the origin, and here the constant c merely shifts that point of centering from the origin to a particular point of interest. If we want the series centered at the origin we merely let $c = 0$. Power series are discussed in standard textbooks such as Hardy (2008 [1908]) and Rosenlicht (1968).

They represent infinite sums; that is, a sum of an infinite number of terms. I know of no precedent for their use in history, historical biology, palaeontology, or archaeology. However they are widely used in the physical sciences. The so-called paths over history technique of quantum field theory, where the vertices of Feynman diagrams are used to consider the evolution of quantum systems via consideration of a power series (Penrose 2004:670-680), is one example. Another example comes from string theory which includes the use of power series in the amplitudes of quantum theory (Penrose 2004:894-896, 909, 943).

I have not said sufficient about z, despite defining a, n and c in (3.1). I said above I would not define z just yet, but I will say one thing here and now. The variable z is chosen to be complex. What does that mean?

There exists a kind of number that turns out to be of fundamental importance in the description of the natural universe (Penrose 2004:67). In fact so important that Penrose (2004) repeatedly refers to them as magic. We call these complex numbers. It will emerge that they can be deployed in the cause of history and anthropology as well, in order to make theory which neatly accounts for certain aspects of the social story I am relating in this book. What are they these numbers, and how do we understand them?

Complex numbers are perhaps easiest to think about through the medium of squares. If we square a positive number we get a positive number (3 X 3 = 9). If we square a negative number we get a positive number (-2 X -2 = 4). So it looks like all square numbers are positive. (Zero just squares to zero so we can ignore that for the moment.) The only concession we have to make to understand complex numbers is to concede that there can exist a number which squares to a negative number, such as -1. We can think of this number as being the square root of minus 1. That is, square root of -1 X square root of -1 = -1. Following the great Carl Friedrich Gauss, the convention is to label this number, the square root of -1, i. So $i^2 = -1$.

This "seemingly mystical quantity", as Penrose (2004:67) calls i, is simply adjoined to the real numbers to give us our complex numbers. That's all there is to it. This allows combinations of i with real numbers to give us numbers of the form

$$x + iy$$

where x and y are real numbers. It is the entire combination that we call a complex number. The $x + iy$ is an entity in and of itself. To remind ourselves of this fact it is best to denote the complex number by another single letter, say z, such that

$$z = x + iy.$$

All the normal rules of arithmetic and algebra are retained by complex numbers. So it seems that what we have to do in order to accept them is not all that much really. But if we do accept them, we reap benefits otherwise unavailable to us through the real number system. For example, according to Penrose (2004:114) power series are often "awkward things" to think about, and our thinking about them using complex variables helps by being "more economical" on the one hand, and providing a "greater depth of understanding" on the other.

As an aside, or a helpful hint concerning complex variables, we can think of a real number x as being a particular case of a complex number $z = x + iy$ when $y = 0$. Then

$$z = x.$$

We can also attempt to visualize complex numbers by thinking of them geometrically. The analogy involves seemingly ordinary Cartesian coordinates, of the kind most of us began to use in elementary third form analytical geometry. An X axis juxtaposed orthogonally with a Y axis. The X axis is conventionally drawn horizontally and goes off to the right of the page infinitely positively. The Y axis is drawn vertically, going up the page infinitely positively.

Now, let us take our complex number in the form $z = x + iy$, and locate it on a pair of coordinates similar to our real numbered Cartesian coordinates. Except that now we will refer to the X axis as the real axis and the Y axis as the imaginary axis. The X axis has units of real numbers as before in the Cartesian universe. But now the Y axis is in units of i, imaginary units.

So we locate our complex number $z = x + iy$ in this space which is no longer Cartesian, but complex. The new space is referred to in most text books as the Argand plane after a mathematician who independently proposed its existence, or simply as the complex plane. Some texts refer to it as Caspar Wessel's plane, after another mathematician whose proposal for its use pre-dated Argand's independent discovery by 9 years.

Location of $z = x + iy$ involves stepping x units along the real axis then climbing y units vertically in the Y direction. This brings us to the point z which has coordinates (x, y) in the Argand plane. The component x, as I said, is called the real part of z while iy is termed the imaginary part of z. And that's all there is to it.

Now that I have revealed and explained the identity of our variable z as a complex variable, let us return to the power series (3.1). Series such as this have three kinds of possible outcomes. One is that the series will converge for all values of z. The second kind diverge for all z except

$z = 0$. And then there is a third kind that converges and then diverges. What do these terms mean?

The best way to consider what we mean by converging and diverging is through examples. Consider the series

$$x^0 + x^1 + x^2 + x^3 ...$$

for $x = 2$. The sum of this grows without limit as

$$1 + 2 + 4 + 8 \, ...$$

so it is called a divergent series. If you could add up all the terms in this series – and there are infinitely many of them – the sum would be infinity. That's divergence.

Alternatively let us consider the series $1/x^n$ for $x = 2$, $n = 1,2,3...$:

$$1/x^1 + 1/x^2 + 1/x^3 + 1/x^4 \, ...$$

or

$$\frac{1}{2} + \frac{1}{4} + \frac{1}{8} + \frac{1}{16} ...$$

which is said to converge to 1. This means the series settles down (Penrose 2004:76-77) to some limiting value, which it gets closer and closer to; in this case 1.

Let us return now to the data of history concerning prostitution. If prostitution is a function of some variable z we saw at the outset of this chapter that it was not possible to locate prostitution in the archaeological, historical or anthropological evidence available for DMP societies. We found definite recorded evidence for prostitution in contemporary texts dating to the most recent 3000 years. (Recall that I also speculated on the period between the origin of VBH societies at about 7000 years ago and that 3000 date, wondering were we looking at an absence of evidence for those 4000 years or evidence of absence.)

So let's think of $f(z)$ in terms of the power series of z. Does it start at the beginning of human history and merely go on growing infinitely? No, it does not. So the history of prostitution and its independent variable is not to be described by a divergent series. Does that history settle down to some limiting value and go nowhere thereafter? In other words, settling down at some DMP type value. No, it does not. For prostitution actually does get going sometime at or before 3000 years before present and grows following that. So the history of prostitution is not to be characterised by a convergent series.

Fortunately, as I said above, we have a third type of outcome for power series. In this case there exists a number r > 0 such that the series converges for all $|(z-c)| < r$, that is, the absolute value of $(z-c)$ is less than r (the vertical bars symbolising absolute value), and diverges for all $|(z-c)| > r$. Possibly the simplest such series, as an example, is given by

$$\sum x^n$$

with $n = 1, 2, 3...$, which converges for $|x| < 1$ then diverges for $|x| \geq 1$. For example, for $|x| = \frac{1}{2}$. the series

$$\frac{1}{2} + \frac{1}{4} + \frac{1}{8} ... \rightarrow 1$$

converges to 1, but for $|x| = 1$ the series

$$1+1+1+... \to \infty$$

diverges.

Such a power series is beautifully applicable to our historical situation. For our social variable z and the function, prostitution, $f(z)$, every time there is change we sum over history such that for all absolute values of $z < r$ the series settles down to a convergent value, a limiting value. Thus we see the situation of the DMP, where the system settled in every historical period without prostitution. Or perhaps there might have even been considerations for getting prostitution going, but these were rejected and the somewhat conservative social system settled back down to the steady as you go situation of traditional history.

Then we see a radical break in history where suddenly, sometime about 3000 years ago or before, we find prostitution extant in VBH societies. The historical sum of events has busted loose, blown out, diverged, brought on something completely new. This theory fits the facts of prostitution's history neatly and exactly.

What's more the theory leads to a pair of predictions, one which comes directly from the above, and the other which I will discuss further presently. The first one is this: as divergent power series sum to infinity, there is an immediate interpretation possible that suggests once prostitution is introduced, invented, got going, it is thereafter headed for infinity; it is unstoppable. Thus this part of the theory predicts the same conclusion reached by different theoretical means in chapter 2.

The value r in the theory above is called the radius of convergence (Rosenlicht 1968:152). This turns out to be of considerable importance to us in regard to the second prediction mentioned above. But before I say more about that we need to consider some other technical issues required to help us with the articulation of this prediction.

DMP to VBH & a measure of hierarchy

Consider a hypothetical terminal Pleistocene/beginning Holocene DMP society S_1 which can be characterized by a set of state variables $s_i, i = 1, 2, 3, ...n$. As S_1 changes into what archaeologists and anthropologists have termed complex society (or in antiquity referred to as civilization), that is what I am calling a VBH society S_2, the s_i take on a different character. Some intensify into new forms, others appear which are radically novel and emergent. Together these constitute the elements of what I have called the VBH set.

Let us further consider the ability to document these changes via an independent variable which is social and cultural. Previously archaeologists have sought to explain these social and cultural changes by means of dependence upon such factors as climate change, warfare, spatial circumscription, etc. More will be said about these in chapter 4. Let us put these aside for the moment, as we do not yet require them for such a hypothetical society as I have posited. (We are supposedly only interested in the onset of prostitution after all.)

This would allow us to characterise these societies, the old and the new, as a function of some key independent social or cultural variable

$$S = f(h) \tag{3.2}$$

where S is the changing society and h is the independent variable. Shortly I will identify this independent variable, but first let us examine the changeover from DMP to VBH societies in terms of the frequency distributions of wealth and possessions available to citizens in a hypothetical example of each kind of society.

In a typical DMP society we find the distribution of wealth and possessions to follow what is called a uniform distribution. That is, each member of the society, given the usual anthropological caveats of age and gender, has about equal access to the resources available to the society at large. That is, the amount of wealth W_i available to the ith individual is given by

$$W_i = W_T / N_T \tag{3.3}$$

where W_T is the total wealth available and N_T is the total number of individuals in the society.

The switch away from DMP to VBH society gives us a social form whose wealth distribution is vastly different from uniform. It follows what is termed a log series (or geometric series) distribution. This is a distribution where a few of the individuals hold most of the wealth, another class or other classes of individuals hold middling to smaller amounts of wealth, and the majority of individuals have little wealth and few means. This is a distribution for societies with relatively small numbers of individuals (as archaeologists tell us the initial VBH societies would have been), but is akin to the log normal distribution that describes wealth distribution in large societies such as those of modern global capitalism. Here in the hypothetical VBH society we see the wealth available to the ith individual is given by

$$W_i = W_T C_k k (1 - k)^{i-1} \tag{3.4}$$

where C_k is a constant of normalization and k is the fraction of total wealth appropriated by the highest ranked individual initially, the fraction of the remaining wealth that is then taken by the second ranked individual, and so on (May 1975). Let us define

$$k(1-k)^{i-1} = G$$

so that we can re-write more (3.4) simply as

$$W_i = W_T C_k G \tag{3.5}$$

The transition from DMP to VBH society is marked by key factors shown in equation (3.3) and (3.5) equation. We see the DMP society characterised by a wealth distribution that goes as $1/N_T$; in other words with approximately egalitarian distribution of resources throughout the society. Whereas the VBH society has the parameter of appropriation G which characterizes its wealth distribution. In other words, wealth concentrated in one individual, with a lesser amount appropriated across the distribution until the great bulk of individuals are seen to have not very big shares at all.

Note that the comparative spread of wealth in the two societies is notionally observed by the two parameters $1/N_T$ and G. The transition from one society to the other is marked by a shift from one to the other key parameter. The dimension of both these can be considered as equivalent to some fraction of wealth (which we can assume to be linked with some measure of power and prestige) per person, which when scanned across the entire probability distribution is what can be seen intuitively as a measure of hierarchy. That is, we can identify the transition as implying

$$\frac{1}{N_T} \to G \Rightarrow h$$

with h as hierarchy. In equation (3.2) I showed an independent variable h. Given the above derivation, this variable can now be considered as hierarchy.

Some other important points we can draw from this relation are: the distributions (3.3) and (3.4) carry with them the implicit invocation that society is increasing is size, in population numbers, from one to the other; another is that as society increases in population size, it draws proportionally greater resources to a comparatively smaller part of the population spectrum; and finally this last also suggests that more resources are being or are capable of being harvested or harnessed by the society whose distribution is given by (3.4). As we will see in the next chapter this has crucial implications for the relation between the product of goods and services harvested, harnessed, etc., to the social structure prevailing.

A second prediction

In relation to the power series (3.1) above I said I would hold off defining the variable z, beyond saying as I did at that time, that it is a complex variable. I will now return to that problem and offer an interpretation, based on the above, for the complex variable z. It is this: the complex variable z can be seen as none other than hierarchy h. However, because it would be computationally useful to have h as a real number, we can view this equality as involving the special case when $y = 0$. When $y = 0$ hierarchy h as equal to the real variable x, such that

$$z = h = x.$$

As I said much earlier in the chapter, the transition from DMP to VBH societies is empirically described well by a power series expansion that converges for $z < r$ then diverges for $z > r$, where that notion r is as described earlier, the radius of convergence in the complex plane. So prostitution can be viewed as a function of the complex variable z which is in turn (for $y = 0$) the real variable derived above: hierarchy h.

Earlier we saw that in the complex plane we have a circle of convergence with radius of convergence r such that for all values of z falling within the circle, the power series converges. Figure 3.1 shows such a circle of convergence, with c being the distance of shift of the circle from the origin, and r the radius of convergence.

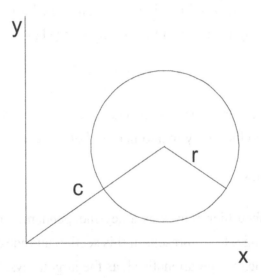

Figure 3.1. The circle of convergence.

This circle of convergence is the DMP of minimal hierarchy and without prostitution. Once we push z outside the circle of convergence, the power series diverges to infinity and gives us not only unstoppable prostitution but an unstoppable VBH set of elements as well (such as king, priests, generals, warfare, …).

Now you may think I am contradicting myself to say an attribute such as {king} is unstoppable, since I characterised the modern USA as a state that had abandoned the idea of king. No. While individual states may so abandon, the idea of kingship globally throughout the VBH world continues unabated. Denmark, Thailand, the United Kingdom are living examples. In fact in some states, and Cambodia is a prime example, the notion {king} has recently been revived, when the ruler Prince Norodom Sihanouk, became King Norodom Sihanouk.

So, to the second prediction. For any given transition from a DMP society to a VBH one, there will exist a value of hierarchy equal to the number r, such that the value of VBH society hierarchy $h > r$. If $h = h_0 < r$ can be considered the value of DMP hierarchy, call it the baseline value, then the VBH hierarchy value h can then be considered as

$$h = \lambda_i h_0$$

where λ_i are some arbitrary coefficients which relate hierarchy in one kind of society to hierarchy in another kind of society.

A hierarchy index

Having established hierarchy h as a key independent variable in DMP VBH social change, I will present in this section an index for h in order for it to be usable, or operationalised, as the jargon says. Such an index allows us to calculate h for various social forms. The method links us back to set theory. There are various ways to think about rank in social systems (White 2007:199-203). This is but one of them. It may not be as sophisticated as native methods such as we see, for example, in Polynesia or on the Northwest Coast of North America, where those who stand closest in a direct line of kinship descent from an exalted ancestor have highest status and rank (White 2007:202). But it works. And, it is easy to calculate.

Sets permit us to talk of vectors, where a vector is a special type of matrix, while a matrix is a rectangular array of elements arranged in rows and columns, then enclosed in brackets. For example

$$A = \begin{bmatrix} a_{11} & a_{12} \\ a_{21} & a_{22} \end{bmatrix}$$

is a matrix A with 2 rows and 2 columns. The elements a_{ij} are arranged such that the subscripts ij represent the row number i and the column number j of each element a. In this case A has 2 rows numbered 1 and 2; the same applies for columns. So the top left hand element of A is a from the first row and first column, hence a_{11}. The top right hand element is in row 1 and column 2, so it is labelled a_{12}; and so on.

A vector is a mathematical object that possesses both magnitude and direction. This is opposed to an object which is determined by a single real number, called a scalar quantity. Examples of scalars include mass, temperature, total runs scored in an innings. On the other hand quantities such as velocity or force have both magnitude and direction, and are vectors. Vectors can be written in several ways (Simmons 1996:600-601), such as in boldface type **v**, or with an arrowhead above $\vec{v}$. If a vector extends from point P to point Q in the plane, we can draw the directed line segment PQ with an arrowhead above it, to label the vector as $\overrightarrow{PQ}$. Yet again a vector can be represented as a special type of matrix, one with either one row or one column. For example, drawing upon the example matrix A above, we could think about a row vector

$$\begin{bmatrix} a_{11} & a_{12} \end{bmatrix}$$

or a column vector

$$\begin{bmatrix} a_{11} \\ a_{21} \end{bmatrix}.$$

To emphasize the difference, I will use a different variable, b, for the column vector, which then becomes

$$\begin{bmatrix} b_{11} \\ b_{21} \end{bmatrix}.$$

An index of hierarchy can then conveniently be given as an operation on two vectors, one a row vector and the other a column vector. This operation is called the dot product of vectors, and is represented for vectors **a** and **b** as

a · b.

That is, two vector quantities **a** and **b**, with the dot between them representing the dot product. So what does this mean, and how do we calculate it?

It turns out that the matrix notation above makes understanding and answering these questions very simple. Taking the example above, the dot product of the row vector and column vector is given by the sum of the products of their various row and column elements.

First we must check that such a product can be performed, that the vectors are compatible for the operation. The rule is: in such a product the number of columns of the first vector must be the same as the number of rows in the second vector. Here we see the number of columns in the row vector is 2, while the number of rows in the column vector is also 2; so the operation can be performed. That is to say, the 1x2 row vector can be "multiplied" by the 2x1 column vector

$$1 \times 2 \, X \, 2 \times 1$$

and an answer obtained. The lower case multiplication signs suggest a 1by2 vector and a 2by1 vector respectively. The upper case multiplication sign in the middle indicates the matrix multiplication operation. The answer, by the way, or at least its form, is given by the outside numerals above. The answer will be a 1x1 matrix, which is to say: it is a scalar quantity; a number.

Now, how to calculate this dot product. We simply take the first element in the row vector and multiply it by the first element in the column vector. We then take the second element in the row vector and multiply it by the second element in the column vector. Then we add these together and we're done:

$$a_{11} \times b_{11} + a_{12} \times b_{21}.$$

Or in shorthand notation, the dot product of the two vectors **a** and **b** is equal to the sum $i,j = 1,2,3...n$ of the respective vector elements:

$$\mathbf{a} \cdot \mathbf{b} = \sum_{i,j}^{n} a_{ij} b_{ij}$$

$$(3.6)$$

And, as I am claiming this gives us a useful and easily calculated hierarchy index, this implies

$$\mathbf{a} \cdot \mathbf{b} = h \qquad (3.7)$$

where h is hierarchy. Note as I flagged above, that such a dot product gives us a scalar quantity. So h is simply a number, a value for hierarchy.

A numerical example

Hierarchy can be seen as related to the distribution of wealth (and with it power and prestige) among individuals in a society. Let us consider a measure of hierarchy that compares the extremes of wealth in such a society, that is, between the wealthiest and the poorest individuals. Imagine the set of attributes that define such individuals. For example, let it have an arbitrary number of elements, where the elements may be such attributes as number of wives (or husbands), financial or material wealth available for personal disposition, area (and value) of property possessed for direct personal use, number of concubines (or royal prostitutes?), number of directly employed servants, number of employees (including government officials and military) directly accountable and answerable, number of slaves directly owned, number of vehicles and other similar accoutrements, presence or absence of divinity or some other elevated religious office, number of temples or other religious buildings constructed by personal wealth or due to prestige, reputation or impetus, length of roads built on similar grounds, irrigation ditches and canals built on similar. Etcetera.

Now let us consider an arbitrary numerical rating over each of these attributes for the particular individuals concerned. Taking what we know from the findings of archaeology, history and anthropology as our guide, let us assign values to various individuals. To return to our analytical notion of vectors, let us consider the above attributes as elements of a vector describing the wealth status of any individual member of the society. Let any given individual be described by a row vector

$$\mathbf{a} = \begin{bmatrix} a_{11} & a_{12} & a_{13} & \cdots & a_{1n} \end{bmatrix}$$

where $\mathbf{a}$ is the vector and the various a_{ij} are the elements representing the above attributes, or a column vector

$$\mathbf{b} = \begin{bmatrix} b_{11} \\ b_{21} \\ b_{31} \\ \cdots \\ b_{n1} \end{bmatrix}$$

structured the same way.

Now, let us take first a hypothetical DMP hunting gathering society where most people have no more wives, husbands, personal wealth, material goods, religious paraphernalia, property, than any other person in the society. They also have no employees, slaves, temples or divine status. For present purposes let us assume that variation due to age and gender in real hunting and gathering societies, such as the number of spouses held my senior men against junior women, or the hunting prowess of adult males against boys, can be ignored for present purposes on the grounds that these do not generally disrupt the kind of hierarchy we are interested in here. In what Sahlins terms the anarchy of DMP societies, let us further assume that on the kind of attributes we are talking about here, people in such a hypothetical DMP society are essentially equal in relation to such attributes.

This implies that in our hypothetical DMP hunting and gathering society the wealthiest and the poorest individual can be given the same numerical ratings for each of the relevant attributes. Let us assign this baseline numerical rating the value 1. So the wealthiest individual in the society can be represented by a row vector

$$\mathbf{a} = \begin{bmatrix} 1 & 1 & 1 & \cdots & 1 \end{bmatrix}$$

across the attributes, while the poorest individual in the society can be represented by a column vector

$$\mathbf{b} = \begin{bmatrix} 1 \\ 1 \\ 1 \\ \dots \\ 1 \end{bmatrix}.$$

Note that I choose 1 as minimum value, as we cannot ever really say that anybody has nothing. Even slaves in their societies have clothes, eating utensils, etc. So a minimum value of 1 represents this having of at least something. This is convenient for the minima also cannot rate zero due to a mathematical property of the vectors: meaning this exercise would fail to show up the hierarchy rating I am attempting to demonstrate.

From (3.6) and (3.7) we see the vector dot product of this to be

$$\mathbf{a} \cdot \mathbf{b} = \begin{bmatrix} 1 & 1 & 1 & \dots & 1 \end{bmatrix} \begin{bmatrix} 1 \\ 1 \\ 1 \\ \dots \\ 1 \end{bmatrix}.$$

Let us assume for ease of example calculation that there are 10 attributes of interest. That is, the row vector and the column vector each have 10 elements. The dot product then gives us the following sum:

$$(1 \times 1) + (1 \times 1) + \dots (1 \times 1) = 10.$$

Which is to say on this occasion, for this DMP hunting gathering society, we obtain the baseline hierarchy value mentioned above:

$$h_0 = 10.$$

Secondly, let us consider another DMP society, also hypothetical, but of the form of those known in historical colonial times on the Northwest Pacific Coast of North America. These so-called Northwest Coast (NWC) societies with names such as Bella Coola, Nootka, Kwakiutl, Tsimshian, lived in relatively high population density, in large groups in villages consisting of wooden plank houses, both residential and ceremonial houses, with elaborate wooden carvings including the famous log totem poles. These people were sea hunters (of large marine mammals) and river salmon fishers. The societies were chiefdoms in which paramount chiefs, hunting chiefs and the so-called potlatch chiefs gained status above the mere ordinary folk. Raids against neighbours were known to produce captives who became slaves. In this sense the societies were somewhat structured into greater hierarchy than we have seen for the first DMP hunting and gathering example.

In what I will call this hypothetical NWC society, rank went roughly from various kinds of chief (paramount, hunting, potlatch) down to slaves, and correlated with status, power, property rights, wives, and so on. However, one caveat is the famous potlatch. Here chiefs worked hard to build surpluses at certain times, but then once attained, this vast pool of wealth (foodstuffs, blankets, perhaps canoes) was given away. Status was gained by the chief, but nothing approaching the wealth acquisition of modern capitalist societies is visible here in this social form.

Let us assign the slave in such a society a numerical value of 1, while we assign the highest status chief with a value of 10. To calculate hierarchy for this NWC society we again follow (3.6) and (3.7). If **a** is the slave vector and **b** the chief vector, we obtain

$$\mathbf{a} \cdot \mathbf{b} = \begin{bmatrix} 1 & 1 & 1 & \dots & 1 \end{bmatrix} \begin{bmatrix} 10 \\ 10 \\ 10 \\ \dots \\ 10 \end{bmatrix}.$$

This calculates out for vectors of 10 elements as

$$(1 \times 10) + (1 \times 10) \dots (1 \times 10) = 100$$

which is to say that for this type of hypothetical NWC society we obtain

$$h_{NWC} = 100.$$

Let us consider finally our hypothetical VBH society. Recall from earlier that VBH societies are marked by attributes such as kings, courts, armies, cities and large towns, bureaucracy, money, writing, monumental architecture, and state based or national religions.

Again, for simplicity of numerical demonstration, let there be minimum and maximum vectors of 10 elements which represent the most wealthy and powerful individual in the society and the poorest most powerless one. That is, we first imagine a vector for the lowliest poorest peasant worker vassal slave, the omega individual in this new VBH society. We rate the elements in this individual's vector as above, at a value of 1 in each case. Consider next a set of attributes of the king, as alpha individual, in this VBH society. Let us rate these for the sake of example, as 100 points each.

To calculate hierarchy for this VBH society we again follow (3.6) and (3.7). If **a** is the slave vector and **b** the king vector, we obtain

$$\mathbf{a \cdot b} = \begin{bmatrix} 1 & 1 & 1 & \dots & 1 \end{bmatrix} \begin{bmatrix} 100 \\ 100 \\ 100 \\ \dots \\ 100 \end{bmatrix}.$$

From this we see that, for vectors of 10 elements,

$$(1 \times 100) + (1 \times 100) + \dots + (1 \times 100) = 1000$$

which is to say that for such a VBH society we see

$$h_{VBH} = 1000.$$

So we arrive at a situation whereby these three hypothetical examples allow us to compare hierarchy across three vastly different societies, illustrating the value of the theory in terms of its usefulness to comparative analysis. The examples will also give us some insight into the vast bigness of hierarchy in VBH societies.

Let us recall the hierarchy values for all 3 societies:

$$h_0 = 10$$
$$h_{NWC} = 100$$
$$h_{VBH} = 1000.$$

If the DMP hunting and gathering society can be considered baseline, the ratio of hierarchy of the NWC society to baseline can be seen from the relation

$$h = \lambda_i h_0$$

to be

$$h_{NWC} = 10h_0$$

with $\lambda_1 = 10$.

Similarly, the VBH society is greater in hierarchy by a factor of 100 in the baseline DMP case, and by a factor of 10 in the NWC case. That is,

$$h_{VBH} = 100h_0$$

$(\lambda_2 = 100)$ and

$$h_{VBH} = 10h_{NWC}$$

where $\lambda_3 = 10$. Note that these λ_i values have the potential to blow up into really big numbers with say, *n* vector elements rather than the simplistic 10 I have used for demonstration purposes. These are merely arbitrary numbers assigned for a simple example. Analysis would involve more carefully worked out assignation of values to well thought out variables for the vectors. The point of this first exercise is to give a simple but clear picture of hierarchy developing exponentially over time with the onset of VBH societies.

It could be argued – successfully, I suggest, as it follows the empirical evidence of history – that VBH societies represent a clean break in hominid evolutionary hierarchy. They are something else again. The world had never known anything on this scale, as big, as extravagant, as ostentatious. The earliest foreign observers at the time of the expansion of European mercantile capital, over the past 500 or perhaps slightly more years, were quick to record (and trash) vast palaces, temples, tombs, walled cities, road networks, bridges, and fortifications, hierarchical societies with vast wealth and power at the top, and desperate lowly poverty and powerlessness at the bottom. Sound familiar?

Before the onset of VBH societies the greatest differences in the hierarchy (and material wealth) of societies would be marked as being between a generalised maximally democratic and egalitarian DMP society on the one hand, and a society akin to the Northwest Coast Indians (NWC) on the other. Remember that NWC is a DMP society too; I choose the acronym as being easier to bring on recall than say DMP_2 or some similar confusing nomenclature. Note that while the ratio of h between NWC and the baseline DMP society is a factor of 10 in my example, the ratio between h values between VBH and NWC is also a factor of 10. But don't be misled. The logarithmic scale associated with these h values needs to be taken into consideration to get a proper perspective on just how big the VBH hierarchy index is in relation to the other social forms.

Due to the log scale these factors of 10 appear to suggest, but most definitely do not imply, equivalence. In terms of the hierarchy index h, this factor of 10 difference between NWC and baseline DMP is actually a difference of

$$h = 100 - 10 = 90 \text{ hierarchy units.}$$

In contrast, the difference between VBH society and baseline DMP $\left(\lambda_2 = 100\right)$ is

$$h = 1000 - 10 = 990 \text{ hierarchy units,}$$

while for VBH to NWC $\left(\lambda_3 = 10\right)$ it is

$$h = 1000 - 100 = 900 \text{ units of hierarchy.}$$

Graphing is one visual technique which shows this effectively (see Clifford & Stephenson 1975:120-122; Chartrand 1985). The above distance relations are graphed in Figure 3.2 as line segments (representing hierarchy units) joining points (representing the 3 societies I have been discussing). The circle shown is the circle of convergence, about which I will say more below. This figure shows clearly that while being greater by a factor of 10 than the baseline DMP society, NWC society is also 90 hierarchy units away from it. VBH society on the other hand, while also being a factor of 10 away from NWC society, is in fact 900 hierarchy units away from the latter. In addition, VBH is 990 units distant from baseline DMP society. It is truly a great leap along the hierarchy index axis from either of the DMP societies to VBH.

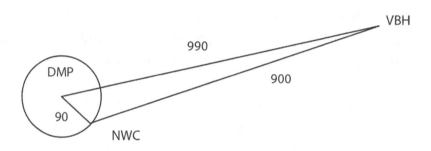

Figure 3.2. Hierarchy relations between DMP, NWC & VBH societies.

For pernickety mathematical reasons NWC cannot lie on the circumference of the circle of convergence. It, like the radius *r*, must sit an infinitesimal distance inside the circumference. This is difficult to draw on this scale so that it is visible to the naked eye. However, mathematical strictness aside, I think Figure 3.2 gives clear insight to see the hierarchical distance between the ultra egalitarian DMP society at the circle's centre and NWC society as the radius of convergence that defines DMP society. It is the maximum separation in hierarchy units, of any two DMP societies. And, as I have shown with my simplified numerical example, it should therefore be possible to obtain a value for this radius (90 units in my simple example) such that we can show precisely all DMP societies lying within the circle of that radius. VBH explodes beyond this circle into very big hierarchy values.

This last point gives great power and beauty to Figure 3.2. It encapsulates dramatically the story of human history. For 6 million years every hominid who strode the planet lived and died in a DMP social context within that circle of convergence. Then when certain forces – be they Rogue Individuals or otherwise – dragged their social structure into a new VBH configuration, these moved vast hierarchical distances away from what had been standard stable normality. Of course in my simple example I show but one generalised VBH setup. The reality is there would be many of these points outside the circle, all different distances away, as VBH societies took slightly variant forms depending on whether they were Urukians, Susans, Egyptians, Akkadians, or Aztecs.

Very well. Having now taken our fairground tour of the hurdy gurdies and horror halls of mathematics, let us return to something completely different: the main theme of this chapter.

When does prostitution begin? 1) Herodotus & history

Let me now look at the implications of all this by beginning to speculate about the beginning of prostitution. When does prostitution begin? Well, already we can say a few things: prostitution has not always been with us, there being no evidence for its existence in DMP societies; it is recorded for various VBH societies from early texts dating to around 3000 years ago; it appears to have existed in every VBH society from its inception until now.

The initial 3000 year ancestry for prostitution in Southwest Asia, Europe and Africa comes to us from Herodotus. The Greek scholar was born in Halicarnassus between 490 and 480 BC, almost some 2500 years before present. He travelled widely in the Greek world, making trips to Egypt and other parts of Africa. He died in 425 BC. He has been called the father of history and the father of anthropology. He indeed can lay claim to both titles. The oral histories he records tell of times hundreds of years prior to his life (some of which tales lapse into the legendary and mythical), his visits to and descriptions of sites such as temples and monuments document the past as an archaeologist might do, and as well, he recorded cultural and social phenomena as he witnessed them during his travels, after the manner of modern ethnography.

He discusses construction of the tomb of the Lydian Alyattes, a monument of stone blocks and earth. It was raised, he tells us, by the joint labour of "tradesmen, craftsmen, and prostitutes" (p.80). On top, and still standing in Herodotus' time, were stone pillars with "inscriptions cut in them to show the amount of work done by each class. Calculations revealed that the prostitutes' share was the largest" (p.80). At that time in Lydia working class girls prostituted themselves without exception to collect money for their dowries, continuing this until they married (p.80).

We witness here first and foremost the existence of prostitution. Moreover, we are given the notion of prostitutes constituting a class, one to be accepted in similar fashion to tradesmen and craftsmen, while it is being respected for its cultural contributions to public life and the memory of the king. But not only accepted and respected, for we see also prostitution as an open and free activity nothing like, for example, the Lesbian prisoner-of-war slaves in chains being forced by their captor Cambyses to dig and construct a moat surrounding the walls of Samos, as he records elsewhere (p.220). Were the prostitutes who worked on Alyattes tomb forced to, as a lower class akin to slaves in chains, surely the ethnographer would have set this down for posterity as he did for the Lesbian example. No such observation is evident. Finally for this initial set of claims, there is the link between prostitution and monumental architecture (albeit a tomb rather than a temple), which is also given mention here.

Discussing the Babylonians, he informs us they deployed "prostitution of all girls of the lower classes" in order to provide some relief from the poverty which followed the Persian conquest "with its attendant hardship and general ruin" (p.121). One of their customs, which he labels "wholly shameful" (p.121), is that every woman must "once in her life go and sit in the temple of Aphrodite and there give herself to a strange man" (p.121). Most "sit in the precinct of the temple" while men wander among them making choices (p.122). No woman is "allowed to go home until a man has thrown a silver coin into her lap and taken her outside to lie with her", she having no choice but to go with this man for sex (p.122).

This is an unusual form of ritual prostitution where each woman prostitutes herself once, and once only, for the sake of the goddess and the temple. This time a more specific link to monumental architecture is noted, indeed to temples themselves. We receive confirmation of prostitution taking place in the temple context. This appears to have been almost universally common. So much so that Herodotus points out the rare (two) cultural exceptions: Egyptian and Greek. It was the Egyptians, he says (p.154), "who first made it an offence against piety to have intercourse with women in temples". "Hardly any nation", he continues, "has any such scruple", as people of most cultures known to him and his peers "constantly see coupling in temples and sacred places" (p.154). Now, as I see it, with pre-marital sex disapproved of, and it seeming highly unlikely a man and his wife would leave home in order to copulate in a temple, the interpretation appearing most likely is that this sex was taking place between temple prostitutes and the male clients who paid donations to said religious site as the price for prostitution.

To return to the unusual case of single time requisite prostitution referred to above. One seemingly innocuous statement requires interpretation, for it may hold import for my later claims. It is this: the woman is "taken outside" for sex. Now at first read this may be glossed as literally taken outside the temple compound. To where? The street? A barn or livery stable? A nearby house? No, I think not. It appears here that he refers to a space outside the main temple area (that he calls "precinct"). This main temple area would of course be devoted to prayer, to offerings, to ritual, in other words the main body of the temple's functioning religious space. Which would seem to imply that his (translated) term "outside" means a place beside the main temple area. I am aware that words such as precinct and outside may reflect a lack of translation clarity, intended meaning lost in translation, and therefore should not be interpreted too pedanticly. Nevertheless, dedicated to the prostitution that occurs there, this "outside" most likely suggests some setup akin to a set of private spaces (such as cubicles or even bedrooms) where the sex events took place.

I purposely use "events" plural. For in proposing such an interpretation, we need to remember that many sex events are most likely occurring concurrently. We are told that there is "a great crowd" of women (p.122) present at such times. Hence it is possible that there were quite a number of these private sex event spaces. There is no reason whatsoever to suspect that such prostitution actually took place in the general modern connotation of "outside", as in meaning out in the open, in the dirt, or on the grass, in full view of everyone. I say this because we are also told of the embarrassment of richer women at having to undertake this ritual sex, driving to the temple "in covered carriages" with servants in tow (p.122). These are wealthy and presumably sophisticated people and acknowledged as such by the ancient researcher. We can easily accept the interpretation that the sex they undertook did not lack couth. For he pointedly contrasts their downplayed understated fornication with the sex habits of others for whom (perhaps in his naiveté) he openly holds in contempt. For example, those who "copulate in the open like wild animals" – people such as the Massagetae (p.122) – or "copulate in the open like cattle" – as he believed the Indian tribes did (p.246). He didn't hold back on such descriptions even if to a modern reader they seem fanciful and misplaced. So if he really meant these temple prostitutes copulated "outside", as in the street or on the lawns, in full view, he would surely have said as much.

On the other hand I cannot imagine these women and their coin tossers standing within the temple precinct in a long queue like World War II Imperial Japanese soldiers, awaiting a turn for the services of their comfort women (Chin Sung Chung 1995:21; Hicks 1997:86,99), literally lined up after work at the door of the one or two small cabins (bedrooms) provided by their logistics people. It does not seem reasonable to imagine lines of temple patrons and their chosen prostitutes queued up waiting for a turn behind the holy pillars or columns, or in some darkened niche behind the altar. I think a dedicated part of the temple with multiple private spaces, probably opening off a corridor or courtyard, is the most likely inference concerning the sites of the actual sex events that comprise the physical component of this prostitution.

As part of a plan to entrap an enemy, we are told of an Egyptian king who "sent his own daughter to a brothel with orders to admit all comers" in order to enact the ruse the king had in mind (p.177). We are told no more about any aspect of the story relevant to my case here. Cheops, another Egyptian king, when short of money, "sent his daughter to a bawdy-house with instructions to charge a certain sum" (p.179). So, we see here references to the existence of prostitution taking place in brothels or bawdy-houses.

However, if analogy be allowed from now to then, brothel means bedrooms. A building with multiple bedrooms, most likely of regimented size and shape (see for analogy Warren 1993:50-52). Or at least some other kind of private space where sex events take place following a meeting or booking in a front space of some kind akin to a reception area or possibly even a meeting site or viewing room. These locations of sex events may be walled, as rooms proper, in a building, or partitioned off in some way (with curtains on runners perhaps, as in many modern massage parlours). Whatever, these constructions also loom as strong possibilities for giving themselves to datable archaeological interpretation if the appropriate variables are searched for. Archaeologists may find in addition to temples, ruins of brothels; perhaps both forms of construction involving these sets of similar rooms or spaces.

On the other hand, we are given mention of the existence in Egypt of both courtesans (the one in question "brought to Egypt" to "follow her trade") and to the more vague and general "prostitutes" (of Naucratis) (p.182). Here we gain an insight into some of the various species of prostitution practised in ancient VBH times, though such references are of no help in adding to the above information suitable for locating archaeological sites where they plied their trade.

So the existence of prostitution as far back as 3000 years before present in VBH society seems well recorded and supported. However, a question we must face about all of this: is Herodotus to be believed? Why do I ask this? Because there seems to be a certain disquiet, even among those such as his twentieth century Penguin Classics editor, who suggests the Hallicarnassan was seen by some as worthy of the descriptor "the father of lies" (Burn, 1988:10). Ancient historian Burn, the editor, also says the Greek failed to appreciate the difference between popular tradition and history (p.10). But surely popular tradition is no more nor less than grist for the mill of anthropology? I would venture that it is and furthermore, qualifies as oral history too. For when it comes to oral history many of us have had difficulties sifting and sorting memories or forgetteries as they might be better called, recollections, distant happenings, from what some positivist might term hard cold facts or truth (Nhuong & Walters 2011; see also Douglas, Roberts & Thompson 1988).

In addition, Herodotus was no linguist and he sometimes appears to have communicated imperfectly (Burn, p.9). He does give us some "strange facts" about distant tribes (Burn, p.10). He was censured by later authors for being "over-credulous" (Burn, p.10). He has his biases, and was at the mercy of his sources (Burn, p.15). Burn (p.238) is at his harshest when Herodotus recounts the speeches made after the killing of the Magi. He says in footnote that these are "obviously fantastic", such that if we wish to pillory him as a liar, here "is the strongest ground."

But on the whole Burn judges him to have been honest, fair, thorough, to have been competent, with charm, a "great lover of his kind" (p.9), tough, a "great pioneer" (p.10), to have used "serious Persian sources", and "made good use of them" (p.22). On the whole Burn's judgment is positive and appreciative. Yes, given the above small caveats, Herodotus is to be believed. And let's face it: many of us are biased, and many of us have been misled by our sources. These go with the territory of the kinds of social, cultural and historical research we try to do. All we can do is attempt always to be transparent about these, to declare the shortcomings as best we understand them, to perhaps provide alternatives, to state the levels of our beliefs. Herodotus does all of this and more.

Of course we can find references to myth, fable and non-fact such as the dolphin carrying Arion on his back to Taenarum (p.49), people copulating in the open, or possessing black semen (p.246), ants bigger than foxes (p.246), flying snakes (p.248). But he takes care to point out where tales are "less rational," even "of a legendary character" (p.137 talking of the

Nile); p.273: "There is a legend ...". We also cannot fail to admire the honesty and fairness that Burn alludes to. We see many disclaimers of a "this is the story as the X tell it" form (p.49 for Corinthians and Lesbians; p.123 for the Massagetae), or "the Y say" (p.114 for the Chaldeans; p.131 for rulers of Egypt), "I know from what I was told" (p.151), "I have relied on the accounts given me" (p.186), "According to the Persians" (p.247), "What they say is" (p.249), "The story goes that" (p.250), "I am told" (p.251), "as I was told" (p.296); "There is a story which I repeat as the Libyans tell it" (p.329).

Or again he points out the several versions of stories he heard (p.130 regarding the Egyptians), and asks if stories have any truth to them (p.173). On p.188 he notes that not only has he taken Egyptian information on their history, but what other people too have had their say on this. "This is one account" he tells us on p.242, but the "Persians also have another"; "According to another account, less generally accepted" (p.253); "The Greeks of Pontus give a different account" (p.273); "... which I consider the most likely of the three" (p.274).

He lets us know the things "I can describe from personal knowledge" (p.96), or "I myself learnt from Z" (p.130 for the Egyptians). And he distinguishes levels of acceptance (p.139: "I speak as an eye-witness, but further south from hearsay"; p.189: "from my own observations ... [or] I can speak of only from report"), "I have no definite information" (p.250), "where [an altar] is still to be seen" (p.262); "a story I heard about him" (p.276); "The remains of [forts] were still to be seen in my day" (p.311).

Accordingly he makes judgments about what he is told, providing his reasoning (p.133 where "I not only believe the people who gave me this account ... but my own conclusions strongly support what they said; p.174 on the version of a story given by the Egyptian priests – "I am inclined to accept it for the following reason ..."; p.177: "I find it hard to believe the priests' account ..."; p.204: "There is also another story current, but not, I think, a convincing one"; p.222: "I think, however, that this is unlikely to be true, because ..."; p.247: "if we may believe the Persians' story" and "It would seem to be a fact"; p.260: "I think myself that"; p.279: "the improbable tale"; "The foregoing measurements were arrived at in the following way" (p.299); "My own view" (p.323).

His bluntness also is striking on such judgments (p.147: "The Greeks have many stories with no basis of fact"; p.181: "I think this story is nonsense"; p.182: "They are quite wrong"; p.204: "The claim ... is not justified by facts"; p.250: "I refuse to believe in one-eyed men"; p.272: "I merely repeat the tradition, and do not myself believe it"; p.284: "a statement which I do not myself believe"; p.306: "I do not believe this tale").

Or alternatively he leaves it to us: "Both stories are told ... the reader may take his choice between them" (p.253), or simply admits defeat: "I was never able to learn exactly" (p.298) or "I imagine, though I do not know for certain" (p.300).

So where do we end up with judgments about the ancient Greek writer? Like his Penguin editor Burn, we all have to acknowledge the flying snakes, the ants as big as foxes, the Indian tribes copulating in the open like cattle, with a wry nod of the head. But we also have to remember that Herodotus was a creature of his times, and in those times the known world was of small boundaries and unlit by empirical investigation, oracles and fanciful ideas abounded, gods were recalled as being actual ancestors; all such expressions carried clout, forming fundamental parts of belief systems.

On the whole however, in my opinion, he emerges as a credible, honest, open, transparent observer and recorder. As seen in the quotes above, he is always willing to separate opinion from actual observation, story from story, certainty from uncertainty, and to rate what he was told as believable or nonsense accordingly.

In particular, I am going to claim that in regard to prostitution and its link with temples, there seems to be no reason to doubt his statements. In addition, there are other records from a similar time period supporting this link. According to Sinha (1993:76) "Secular prostitution in India dates back to Vedic times." The Vedic period of subcontinental history is dated approximately from 1500 BC to 500 BC (Wikipedia). That is, from 3500 to 2500 years before present give or take. The Vedic empire was located in northwest India. Its earliest text, claimed to have been written around 3000 years ago, is known as the Rigveda. Presumably, though not cited specifically, this is Sinha's reference source. And while its records involved secular prostitution, which is itself interesting for its match with Herodotus' records of brothels and bawdy-houses, temple prostitution also took place.

> Prostitutes were very much a part of the Vedic society...
> They came to be known as 'devadasis' – the girls who
> were married to God in a temple and expected to spend
> the rest of the life as his maid serving the men in the
> society.

> http://hinduism.about.com/od/history/a/vedic_women.htm

Sinha (1993) also notes the presence of these devadasis, while providing the English equivalent term: "temple girls" (p.78). Elsewhere, sourcing the Mahabharata (time?) he talks of "temple harlots" (pp.71-2).

Below I will use this ancient historical information linking prostitution to temples to set up a hypothesis leading to a prediction. Along the way, as will be seen, I return briefly to set theory, making a suggestion for, or a plea to, mathematicians to help out. For if readers will accept, as I do, the records of Herodotus and other writers of the times, then allow this one last bit of theory, we are presented with an opportunity to predict the onset of prostitution in such a way that it can be sought in the archaeological record.

When does prostitution begin? 2) hypothesis & prediction

In regard to the onset of prostitution my suggestion earlier in this chapter was to consider two possibilities: one being that prostitution really did get going only around 3000 BP; which means we are left with explaining why it was not present from the beginning of VBH societies at say 7000 years ago, why it took 4000 years to come into being, and why it did at that time and after that time appear universally throughout the VBH world? The second possibility is that it came into being along with the rest of the VBH set at the origin of VBH societies some 7000 years ago but remained historically and archaeologically invisible until it was recorded for us by scribes with the onset of writing 4000 years later.

Is there any theory that might help us decide the issue? Unfortunately no, there is not. Or at least, none that I am aware of. But is there any way we could explore this void of theory to help us out? Possibly, but it takes us into territory where any suggestion I make risks being dismissed as the outpourings of an amateur interloper. Nevertheless, like Edward Said (1994:65), I do not consider myself bound by my professional training, hence "speak and write about broader matters because as a rank amateur I am spurred on by commitments that go well beyond my narrow professional career." So to my suggestion. And the suggestion, it seems to me, implies that it would require new developments in mathematics.

Very well; amateur interloper I may well be. But nevertheless, let me sketch out briefly the kind of ideas that such a theory might consist of. My idea involves a return to set theory which we encountered earlier in the chapter. Unfortunately it demands an entry into rules for elements of sets which, as far as I am aware, do not exist. To try to explain what I mean, let us consider an example. If we encounter the set of DNA bases {B}, and we are told that two elements of that set are the elements adenine and guanine, then we know immediately that there must be two more elements and the names of the elements must be thymine and cytosine. These additional elements are required by obligation, given the definition demanded by the name of the set they belong to.

Consider another example: toss outcomes for a fair coin of normal minting. If we have a set {C} named sides of a coin, and we are told that one element of the set is called heads, we know immediately the set must consist of 2 elements and the second hidden element must be called tails. Generalise this with another example: the set of outcomes of a Bernoulli trial {O}: if we are told one element of that set is called success, we know immediately that the set consists of 2 elements with the hidden second element being called failure. One final example: if we encounter a set of primary colours of the rainbow, the spectrum of white light, {R}, and we are informed that the set has visible elements red, orange, yellow, we know immediately that the set must have 7 elements with the remaining hidden elements being called: green, blue, indigo, violet.

On a slightly different tack White (2007:202) reminded us that "no one can be a king without subjects. A mass of commoners is necessarily implied by a class of great chiefs or nobles." Each element is obligate upon the other, much in the manner I have suggested for the above sets.

I will suggest that such a set has elements which are obliged to be there, to accompany the given elements, by virtue of the definition (name chosen) of the set. Were I to have the temerity to make suggestions to mathematicians, I would offer the tentative idea that we might term such sets obligate sets. We could define an obligate set as a set that has a required number of necessary elements, dependent upon how the set itself was defined. That is, if we define a set as being the primary colours of the rainbow, we know straight away that it must contain 7 elements. We also know the names of these elements completely.

More formally, if we have a set $\{B_T\}$ that must contain T elements, and we know that $\{B_T\}$ contains given elements $\{b_i, i = 1, 2, 3...m, m < T\}$, such that to fit the definition of $\{B_T\}$ the only possibility for the remaining elements of $\{B_T\}$ has to be $b_j, j = m+1, m+2...T$, then we can call $\{B_T\}$ an obligate set.

To me, the proof of such a statement seems so obvious that it must surely be simple and straightforward for mathematicians. For if we define a set as a set of the type $\{B_T\}$ (for example the outcomes of a fair coin toss) and state some number of the given elements, say, {heads, ...} then assume that the remaining elements are not equal to b_j, (for example, the remaining elements are not equal to 1, i.e. tails), this leads to a contradiction (that there is only one outcome, heads (a one-sided coin), or there are more than 2 outcomes (3 for example, heads, tails, zebra). Both of these results are clearly absurd and lead to contradiction. So by contradiction, the statement is proven.

Now, were we allowed to do such a thing, to make such a mathematical invention, then as theory it is beautifully suited to my purposes here.

I merely define the VBH set as an obligate set and suggest the visible elements: king, prince, general, priest. I know by inference from all the empirical evidence we have for VBH societies from and after 3000 BP, that prostitution becomes an obligate element in such a set.

Such a theory then would help us in laying down some kind of rule for the beginnings of prostitution at the same time as the onset of VBH societies: 7000 years ago give or take. The challenge to field archaeologists would then be: can you operationalise variables that would allow you to find evidence for prostitution in your sites from that earliest VBH period?

What kinds of data might archaeologists use to test such a hypothesis? As I see this issue it requires at least a small leap of faith towards what might be deemed operationalised variables. Or rather, two leaps, one from each of opposite directions. Where those variables are to do with bedrooms.

The first leap comes from contemporary ethnography, or is at least inspired by it. In Walters (2013) I raised a hypothesis concerning the onset of use of bedrooms for sex as being intimately connected with hotels and whorehouses. The hypothesis emerged from thinking about hotels and their crucial use in contemporary prostitution in Vietnam, a use I had recorded ethnographically (Walters 2013). It concerns the development of the bedroom as a site for private sex (as opposed to being simply a space for sleeping), via constructions such as hotels and brothels. The hypothesis (following Walters 2013) requires a brief introductory spiel on cross cultural sleeping arrangements, on a thin slice of Vietnamese history, and on the hotel as a sexual space.

Hotel rooms are essentially spaces for sleeping and private sexual activity. Of course they have other roles: bathing, toileting, writing on a laptop, conducting private phone conversations, conducting business meetings, parties. But their main place in the world is to allow privacy in those two key acts. That is, at base they are bedrooms.

Now, when we look deeper into the structural and historical notions of these activities in relation to bedrooms we arrive at some interesting findings. A large fraction of the world's cultures, past and present, do not employ the notion of bedroom to undertake these key activities. For example, the entire suite of (DMP) Indigenous Australian cultures prior to European invasion of their continent, as far as is known, decoupled sleeping and sexual activities. Sometimes men slept with their wives, though just as frequently many ethnographically recorded cultural situations reveal men sleeping with other men, such as their brothers, uncles, nephews, or their sons. Wives slept with their co-wives, sisters, aunties, mothers, daughters. Sexual activity took place in secret, during bush foraging or collecting activities, "in the long grass" as some modern Indigenous Australians like to say in English. Sometimes at night, mostly in the daytime, while children and other potentially disturbing factors were being managed by grandmothers, aunties, and so on, men and women fornicated in private, but in the "long grass."

Another example of similar DMP style: in many Melanesian societies, men slept (and sleep) in men's houses, with their male kinfolk, while women slept at home with their children and pigs. Sexual activity between a man and his wife, or indeed between lovers, took place in gardens or in the bush, while people were formally engaged in the daily toil of gardening or hunting. No role for bedrooms.

One further example: In contemporary Vietnamese families with which I am familiar men both do and do not sleep with their wives. When they do, and when children are asleep or ensconced in another bed or room, sexual activity can take place. When they do not, they visit each other's bed during private times when sex is required. Here too, as often as not, men sleep with their sons, wives alone or with daughters.

Here we recognise no concept of bedroom that universally involves both a) sleeping with your heterosexual partner, and b) undertaking private sexual activity. This last seems on the face of it to be a largely Indo-European idea, at least in recorded history and modern times. Obviously then, transliterated by colonialism to other cultural contexts.

A quick skim over the surface of Vietnamese ancient history and prehistory brings us to what might be termed the medieval equivalent, or middle ages equivalent. It takes us to a time of European mercantile contact, and even settlement on the coast of Vietnam at places like Da Nang and Hoi An. Chinese and Japanese traders also established beachheads in these places at the same time. Vessels from the Mediterranean plied their wares onto the Vietnamese and Cambodian coasts. Indian and other missionaries were travelling around the region proselytizing Buddhism, French and other Christians were trying for a similar competitive philosophical foothold. For while this part of the world, aptly known as Indo-China, has been a meeting point of vigorous trade for a long time, with east Asians coming from the north and the Indians, western Asians and Europeans coming from the west, landscapes were now becoming more familiar to modern understandings. Large towns and cities began to develop as entrepots, markets and ports. Roads and other infrastructure would have increased in number and size. New religions and languages appeared and became domesticated. A money economy was introduced.

It is during this time then that Barbara Watson Andaya sets her powerfully attractive hypothesis (referred to earlier in the chapter). Prostitution takes on a new sensibility, according to Andaya (and Reid as well – see earlier) suggesting that whore work was displacing the older more positively viewed category of temporary wife. But whore work had to have somewhere to undertake the actual sexual activity. For temporary wives and concubines it had been easy: they ensconced themselves serially with their merchant "husbands" in houses or apartments. But other kinds of sex work (whore work) demand a venue, and often a neutral one at that.

Brothels are one obvious answer, but hotels are another. Whichever, and whatever other establishments were utilised, they would also have been founded upon the bedroom as the site of private sexuality. This is the big change that I saw in regard to thinking about the role of modern hotels in prostitution (Walters 2013). A culture, given what we might choose to infer from its archaeological heritage and from its history of peasantry and rural residence, that was without the idea of a bedroom as a place of both sexual action and sleeping, changes to adopt and deploy such an idea. Hotel prostitution begins. That is, publicly utilised bedrooms, rented for private purposes, take a new role in commercial sexual activity. Whorehouses, brothels and hotels came to have multiple bedrooms set adjacent, of similar size and design. Is this what Herodotus is implying for his 3000 year old temples and their prostitution? Recall the "outside" discussion above where I suggested such spaces, used for multiple private sex events, were part of the temple complex. But even more tellingly: did the earliest VBH temples do likewise?

Archaeologists might search for such structural arrangements in early VBH towns and cities. Or, and this brings me to the second leap of faith: temples and their role in prostitution. If we were willing to accept that the earliest, or some of the earliest recorded prostitution took place in temples, as described by Herodotus from 3000 years ago and cited repeatedly in secondary sources (Scott 1996 [1968], Sinha 1993, Goodall 1995), then the many temple sites at the ruins of the earliest VBH towns and cities may contain valuable evidence. As above, I am thinking of structures such as barrack style bedrooms adjacent the main prayer and ritual areas of the building, used by priestesses of the temple (as Scott calls them – i.e. prostitutes) for the sex work which led to client donations to the temple. So the archaeological variables might be to do with these bedrooms being smallish, of similar size and shape, arranged side by side, hotel-like, containing minimal accoutrements beyond things like a sleeping (a euphemism) platform, clothes rack, hanging cupboards. Sinha (1993:69) shows a comb which he claims belonged to a prostitute. Other possibilities come to mind: containers for prophylactics, washing bowls, douche materials. Such artefacts, if found in these rooms, may also be useful for archaeological inference.

Let me take this more formally to a prediction. I suggest my ideas predict the presence in earliest VBH temples, of such material culture: rows or other arrangements of smallish, similar sized and shaped rooms with sleeping platforms, as well as the potential presence of small items for personal care or beauty care, or for aiding and abetting sex events.

Summary & Conclusions

No historic or ethnographic, much less archaeological literature reveals evidence for prostitution prior to the Recent development of VBH societies. Then when it does appear in those societies it is suddenly ubiquitous. Though first known records of prostitution date to around 3000 years ago, appearing in the writings of Herodotus, it may be that the gap between onset of VBH social forms and prostitution is merely a function of the latter needing to await the invention of writing to have its initial presence recorded for posterity.

DMP and VBH societies are briefly characterised. The former appear to have been with us for 6 million years, while the latter are Recent phenomena, perhaps 6000 years old, maybe 7000. The former are characterised by the priority of culture and society, via domestic groups, while the latter are surplus driven, with elite groups and individuals cranking the economic system up. VBH societies are all about the economy [stupid], and profit motives, while in the DMP underproduction is the norm and profit concerns don't rate.

Set theory is introduced to describe the beginnings of VBH lifeways via what I term the VBH set. This is found to characterise social history nicely. It shows for example, attributes of social structure dropping out of use or relevance over time, often as a result of being replaced by new forms. Particular use is made of what is known in set theory as the von Neumann constructible universe. This shows in our case here, that varied cultures were free to pick and choose their own attributes, making them vastly diverse over time and space. This aspect of the theory also suggests that the general picture of nearly six million years of hunting and gathering is a tapestry of cumulative cultural pattern.

However, I argued there is no implication here of progress, or that each and every culture is required to pass along the same linear path. Rather, the theory carries implications for the broad sweep of global culture. History and theory are aligned: things change over time, with a general human cumulative accretion of cultural traits.

Another feature of this part of the theory is that there is no going back. As with a cumulative collection of additive sets, addition of culture traits in general does not change direction, there is no reversion. Where a cultural trait is withdrawn from a social structure, where there is a subtraction, an abandonment, equivalence holds good, such that there is no structural reversion.

The chapter also showed the theory predicts the absence in hominid history of any possible reversion such as utopian anarchy (as opposed to DMP anarchy). There will not be an abandonment of government, of the law, of the kinds of hierarchically collective action that leads to armies, cities, and the like. Mind you, if it ever does happen, my theory is rejected. Or at least this aspect of the theory.

However, the theory tells us more. As I said above in the text of the chapter, VBH societies mark a discontinuity in human history. With VBH societies we see the addition of what I now refer to throughout this chapter and the book as the VBH set. This is the set of sets that define VBH societies as a completely new phenomenon on planet Earth. Never before in the history of our world or the evolution of life on it has anything like it occurred. The VBH set contains elements of the kind: {king, court, bureaucracy, army, class, appropriated surplus, writing, numeracy, ...}.

In the broad sweep of hominid history, if ever, and if so wherever and whenever, attributes which eventually became the VBH set threatened to arise singly or in a multi-element set, they were quickly repudiated, rejected, killed off (perhaps literally) before they had a chance to take root. They may have been diverted into something culturally and politically acceptable to societies of their times. Whatever, we can be sure that for almost six million years since we separated from our common ape ancestor, no VBH set arose. Until it did, that is, in some particular parts of the world in the Recent period.

I then turned to theory on the construction of the VBH set. Beginning with V_0 = the empty set, {}, we eventually ended up with the set noted above: {king, court, bureaucracy, army, class, appropriated surplus, writing, numeracy, ...}.

Then I took another theoretical step, to consider history as a power series. That is, to consider some historical variable of interest which I called z .

As we would expect for history, z is changing over time. I then suggested another variable of interest which depends on z and changes in accord with it, which I called $f(z)$. That is, some function of z. Because that's what this book and the theory are about, this latter variable I said we should call prostitution.

I also suggested we are on the side of the angels if we choose to use complex variables. I proceeded to show what these are, and combined with the efficacy of power series, began a demonstration of their usefulness to my theory.

The central useful point of all this was to show that power series have three kinds of possible outcomes. One is that the series will converge for all values of z. The second kind diverge for all z except $z = 0$. And then there is a third kind that converges and then diverges.

This last option is, I suggested, applicable to the historical situation. For our social variable z and the function, prostitution, $f(z)$, every time there is change we sum over history such that for all absolute values of $z < r$ the series settles down to a convergent value, a limiting value. Thus we see the situation of the DMP, where the system settled in every historical period without prostitution. Or perhaps there might have even been considerations for getting prostitution going, but these were rejected and the somewhat conservative social system settled back down to the steady as you go situation of traditional history. Then we see a radical break in history where suddenly, sometime about 3000 years ago or before, we find prostitution extant in VBH societies. In this theoretical view, the historical sum of events has busted loose, diverged, brought on something completely new. This describes the historical record of prostitution neatly and exactly.

The theory leads, as I said above, to a pair of predictions. Firstly, as divergent power series sum to infinity, there is an immediate interpretation possible that suggests once prostitution is introduced invented got going, it is thereafter headed for infinity; it is unstoppable. Thus this part of the theory predicts the same conclusion reached by different theoretical means in chapter 2. Secondly, for any given transition from a DMP society to a VBH one, there will exist a value of hierarchy equal to the number r, such that the value of VBH society hierarchy $h > r$. If $h = h_0$ $< r$ can be considered the value of DMP hierarchy, call it the baseline value, then the VBH hierarchy value h can then be considered as $h = \lambda_i h_0$, where λ_i are some arbitrary coefficients which relate hierarchy in one kind of society to hierarchy in another kind of society.

In the meantime, above in the text of the chapter I had discussed this variable hierarchy, h. The transition from DMP to VBH society is characterised by a change in wealth distribution that goes from an approximately egalitarian distribution of resources throughout the society to one that has an appropriation parameter which characterizes its wealth distribution. Then I noted that the comparison of spread of wealth in the two societies is notionally equivalent to some fraction of wealth (which we can assume to be linked with some measure of power and prestige) per person, which when scanned across the entire probability distribution is what can be seen intuitively as a measure of hierarchy, h.

Having arrived at hierarchy h as a key independent variable in DMP to VBH social change, I then presented an index for h in order for it to be a practical variable of use. The index allows calculation of h for various social forms. The method thus links us back to set theory. After that I gave a simple numerical example to show how such an index works for various hypothetical societies, both DMP and VBH.

Then the chapter switched to history, principally the accounts of prostitution from the time when writing comes into the archaeological record. I provided a set of quotes and references from Herodotus, writing of the Greek world in the period 3000 to about 2400 years ago. These were augmented by a small number of other sources as well. The major outcome of my examination of this work is to conclude that from about 3000 BP at least, there is a strong presence of prostitution in temples, with sex work also practised more secularly in brothels.

The final section of the chapter discusses the implications of this historical finding for what might be found archaeologically. A prediction is arrived at that prostitution began some 7000 years or so ago with the onset of VBH societies, and that with luck and appropriate variables examined, its presence might be found in the ruins of ancient sites from this time.

CHAPTER 4

Implications of the theory

I have shown theoretically how prostitution, once begun, is unstoppable. I have also proposed a theory for prostitution beginning in the early Holocene period with the onset of Very Big Hierarchy (VBH) societies. As I said at the outset, my theory covers both ends of the function that is prostitution.

But so what? Those who have an interest of academic sorts in sex work research do not seem to be interested in theory. And the few who might be would most likely have interest in neither the deep past nor archaeology, so will care little for my predictions and conjectures. (Many in the more popular literature will go on blithely claiming prostitution as the oldest profession, a social evil or necessity that has been with us humans always – whatever the unexplained always means.) Then again, I cannot imagine too many archaeologists who would give a fig about prostitution, whether that involves claims about its beginnings or otherwise.

Is there anyone then, who might find some interest in my theory? Perhaps if I show that it has several real world applications it may catch the attention of a few. But which few? Well, the only implications that leap

114

out at me at present are threefold, and all involve issues which have been prominent in archaeology and anthropology since grave robbing times. Archaeologists have pondered, for example, the origins of what they usually termed civilization, for more than a hundred years. Social scholars – some of whom we may claim for anthropology – have as well.

The downside of such origins is the collapse of those very same societies, the ones I am referring to in this work as Very Big Hierarchy societies. A body of research exists dedicated to this very topic. Almost all of that literature, as far as I know, is archaeological. So perhaps here is another real world problem that may interest at least some scholars.

Thirdly, there is the relation first raised by Leslie White in the 1940s, between cultural development – as he called it – and energy harnessing. Now, maybe this is an issue that still holds some interest for both anthropologists and archaeologists. For the latter it appears to have been interesting up till the turn of the millennium anyhow (Wenke 1999). Perhaps it still is.

This chapter then, presents some comments and remarks of a theoretical bent about these three issues. My aim is not only to have something to say about them which may have some value, but also to show how my little theory about the ends of the prostitution function may have some real world interest. I begin with an overview of ideas about origins of VBH societies. Drawing upon my own theory, I then intrude some remarks about how a transition to VBH societies may have come about. This is followed by a section on the demise of said societies, and what implications the theory contains for this. Finally I address the White relation.

Drama after the Ice

There is an old saying in roulette: never bet against the wheel. When the run is red, wisdom says bet red. When it switches, as it does, to black, that same received wisdom says bet black. In similar fashion an observer (extra-terrestrial or whatever) capable of looking at 6 million years of the hominid record would have been seriously deluded to think of betting against the wheel of human history. Which is to say, the metaphorical run was with hunting and gathering. That same observer could have been forgiven for thinking the hominid world of hunting and gathering would have gone on forever. No pan-historic observer in their right mind, checking out a global snapshot at say, 20,000 years ago or just before, would have bet against the wheel, on the sudden dramatic changes of the early Holocene in Southwest Asia, and all else that followed thereafter.

But, there you go. It happened. Six million years of hominid hunting and gathering, predominantly in small bands, began to be rapidly confronted by peoples who planted, harvested and stored grain, as well as domesticating a number of animal species for consumption and use as machines. They reaped the surpluses generated by these new economic pursuits. They congregated in towns some of which became cities. They engaged in vast construction projects involving temples, monuments, irrigation systems, fortifications. And, which is most important, they gave up largely democratic social systems (anarchic, as Marshall Sahlins calls them) to work for, die for, and show allegiance to nodal individuals who had accrued vast wealth, power and influence. This all happened, give or take, as the Pleistocene Ice Age receded, world climate ameliorated, and some areas of the temperate northern hemisphere witnessed the spread of species of grasses whose seeds would prove crucial in the dramatic changes that consequently took place in cultures and societies. Within ten thousand short years – roughly order of magnitude one thousandth of hominid history - the world would look like the one in which we now live. A world so breathtakingly different from what had gone before that no hunter from 20,000 years ago, resurrected and time travelled to witness, would ever believe.

Just before agriculture, during the terminal Pleistocene, the archaeological record shows people in Southwest Asia had: begun trading more; had begun to develop material culture markers of status differentiation; had become more aware of ethnic identity as revealed by ubiquitously distributed marker artefacts, especially certain kinds of ceramics; and even though they were continuing to hunt and gather, had begun to undertake horticulture and agriculture as well; and they had begun storing leftover food products (Wenke 1999:286).

Then in one short but dramatic burst we see what archaeologists interpret as societies organised into a class structure, one or some of whom exude and deploy the advantages of inherited privilege while, as elites, they engaged in exploitation of the masses. We see evidence of warfare on a scale never known by hunting societies, pastoral nomads or hunter horticulturalists. Many cities became fortified, with diabolical weapons of war invented and put to use. Killing on a grand scale, that is, human slaughter, became the invented prerogative of so-called civilization. Monuments, tombs, and grand buildings were constructed, mostly in a manner described by modern archaeologists as wasteful – of resources and manpower. Belief systems of a local variety give over to what can be described as national religions (ideologies that sanction across empires). Eventually we see writing discovered.

The "earliest true writing" appears "quite suddenly" during the Jemdet Nasr phase in Mesopotamia around 5100 to 5000 BP (Gowlett 1984:182). Similar systems appear around the same time or just after in both Iran and Egypt. Its decidedly later appearance, by several hundred years, in the Indus and China, suggests to Gowlett (1984:182) "that the idea had been transmitted" from Southwest Asia. Alternatively, the "earliest known written documents" from Uruk dated at 5400 BP have 1,500 symbols (carpenter, boat, etc.), including a standard professions list (Wenke 1999:413) (I ask: any temple whores mentioned as a profession?). Women appear to have been "reasonably well treated" by law and custom in Sumerian society, despite it being "strongly patriarchal" (Wenke 1999:418). So if prostitutes were mentioned, they would presumably not have been sullied or swept under metaphorical carpets as in modern times. We also see Sumerian ration lists, work forces, guild lists, snake charmers; all are recorded (Wenke 1999:419).

Archaeologists seem to be suggesting that it is not until we have writing and widespread urbanism that we have civilization, aka VBH societies. Now this in turn implies that the VBH set, as I introduced it in chapter 3, would have come together somewhat piecemeal over a 2000 year development phase, culminating in the use of writing some 5000 years ago. (Further this may lend support to a relatively late arrival of prostitution.) But I would argue against such thinking. Theory seems to suggest that a phenomenon like the VBH set arrives full blown, especially if we allow my conjectured obligate sets (see chapter 3).

However, civilization "cannot be rigorously defined" (Gowlett 1984:6). And, as is well known, these social forms "arose, not once, but time and again in very different circumstances" (Gowlett 1984:172). My theory is at ease with this, for it does not in any way suggest all VBH societies got going at the same time. What it does mean is that once the transformation is in place, whatever the timing, whatever the location, the VBH set follows rapidly, immediately in an archaeological or historical sense of visibility. This in turn has implications: either we abandon writing from the obligate VBH set (urbanism is well in place), or if we argue it must be admitted, predict that its beginnings came on perishable materials (these could even be ephemera like sand scrawls) while our hard evidence for it only comes later.

Returning now to the above attributes, most of which are those ancient historians, Egyptologists, and archaeologists consider to be markers of these new social forms. In the early days of research, looting and grave robbing, this whole phenomenon was thought about in terms of the origins of civilization. In more recent decades archaeologists have tended to temper and generalise their descriptors, referring to such phenomena as complex societies. For reasons detailed in my theory, I have introduced in this book the notion of Very Big Hierarchy (VBH) societies. Let's look at some examples.

The Uruk period 5600-5000 years Before Present (BP) has "the complete checklist of civilization: cities, warfare, writing, social hierarchies, advanced arts and crafts, and other elements" (Wenke 1999:404) That there are unnamed "other elements" ensures this is not in fact the complete list. Nevertheless, it gives us some idea. For China after 4000 BP "all the correlates of cultural complexity, such as monumental architecture, large population concentrations, occupational specialization, written records, gross differences in wealth, power, and prestige, and large public-works projects" are in place (Wenke 1999:523).

Archaeologists tell us that by 5000 years ago Uruk housed some 50,000 people behind substantial defensive walls. Among them "kings, priests, scribes, farmers, soldiers, slaves, etc." (Wenke 1999:406). Documents written about 4600 BP talk of conflict between the people of Uruk, those of Ur, Umma, and other city-states.

The "initial stimulus" for urbanisation at this time seems related to "defensive needs", imposed by a "small, politically conscious superstratum" motivated principally by military and economic interests (Wenke 1999:406). Robert Wenke quotes Gregory Johnson saying a "series of emergences" of "individual states in a network of politics" is evident by this time (Wenke 1999:408). By 5200 BP conflict between the elites of Susa and those of Chuga Mish reflects an attempt by the latter to sever its dependent relationship on the former. Between 5,000 BP and 4350 BP Sumeria has some 13 city-states (Wenke 1999:412).

In passing, while mentioning Sumeria, Gregory Johnson used rank-size distribution to demonstrate the pattern for settlement size in Susiana (Sumeria). That is, he found many smaller sized settlements with smaller and smaller numbers of ever larger towns and cities. But, Wenke (1999:409) claims, "no one really knows what the different kinds of rank-size plots mean." For they "are essentially empirical generalizations without any theory to explain them" (Wenke 1999:409). But this is mistaken. The distribution Johnson detected reflects hierarchy, with settlement size showing the same kind of pattern as distributions of individual wealth, and other indicators of VBH societies. For example, in Sumeria we note the following hierarchical elements: god-king, nobles, wealthy businessmen, scribes, artisans, smiths, slaves (Wenke 1999:419). In China: king (with supernatural powers), hierarchically arranged nobility, commoners. As far as theory goes, beyond the key role for hierarchy, the mathematics of statistical theory accounts for such distributions in a straightforward manner. As I showed in chapter 3, once frequency distributions grow large and assemble the way VBH variables do, we expect (and presumably Johnson found) the distributions to be log normal.

Back to the travelogue. Eridu had temples at 7000 BP or so. In chapter 3 I conjectured on the role of these in prostitution. By about 5000 BP Uruk has several large temples, a diversion of enormous amounts of energy into the building of those temples, pyramids, and other monuments (Wenke 1999:410). Later (below) I will offer a possible interpretation of why this is so, accompanied by a prediction.

After 5000 BP there was "almost constant warfare" in Sumeria (Wenke 1999:420). After 4450 BP quarrels among rival claimants (Akkadia) saw the "state fragmented" (Wenke 1999:422). At 4100 BP another king was able to stabilize things, to re-establish control as the Ur III dynasty (Wenke 1999:422). Ur III goes under however, by 4004 BP, with invasion by the Elamites from western Iran; the king of Ur being captured. From 4000 BP to 3800 BP Greater Mesopotamia fragmented yet again, as various kings "established contending states" (Wenke 1999:422). By 3792 BP Hanumurabi established the Babylonian empire. The "many documents of his reign ... reflect a skilful politician" (Wenke 1999:423).

In Egypt hundreds of unconnected and similar villages transmuted into the state (Wenke 1999:445-6), from about 6000 BP in the south, then by 5000 years ago, all over the country. In China and at many places across the Old World stratification of wealth and power, detectable in the distribution of grave goods, becomes evident once settled villages appear (Gowlett 1984:167).

A general summary then would correlate many variables with the rise of VBH societies. To begin a list, we must mention: surpluses, population growth, warfare, agriculture, developments in technology. Sedentary communities abound. And of course, there is hierarchy. For "wherever there is plentiful and reliable food ... our ancestors have responded in one way ... exaggerate differences ... in access to wealth, power, and privilege" (Wenke 1999:274). "Throughout the world, inequalities in wealth, power, and prestige seem to have grown ever greater through history" (Wenke 1999:331). And "wherever one finds economic systems that produce great surpluses, one also discovers elaborate social hierarchies" (Wenke 1999:424).

The "connection between energy and culture is close and causal" (Wenke 1999:566). The "greater the amount of energy a culture can capture and efficiently utilize, the better its competitive chances" (Wenke 1999:347).

Then we begin to see suggestions of possible causality. We see that "great amounts of food ... allows population densities to rise" (Wenke 1999:274). Social "power was derived from control of agricultural production" (Wenke 1999:333). "As in all the other cases ... aspects of economy, ecology, and demography explain much of what happened" (Wenke 1999:609).

Northern European scholars and adventurers, appearing to be the only people seriously interested in archaeology at the time of the expansion of mercantile capitalism, declared all this to constitute the onset of what they called civilization. They postulated direct links of cultural lineage between the early civilizations at the eastern end of the Mediterranean busily being uncovered by excavations, surveys and looting, and their own eighteenth and nineteenth century societies. Such thinking persisted into the twentieth century and continues today.

The Europeans deemed themselves the world's most progressive societies, based on measures which their countries and cultures possessed. In this tautology if society *A* had attribute *a* it was a sign of progress, and because of the presence of *a*, society *A* must therefore be the most progressive, the most advanced, the most developed, the highest civilization. Which is to say, at the top of the pyramid of social evolution. Nineteenth century scholars fell in rapture with the stage concept. They told a world history based on stages of first Savagery, followed by Barbarism, then finally, for some cultures at least, Civilization. Many other key attributes were selected to fit this scheme. Northern European languages were judged the most developed, followed by those spoken in barbaric and savage speech communities. The religions of northern Europe were seen as the belief systems most advanced (Christianity and Judaism), while barbarians possessed Islam, Confucianism, Buddhism, and the like. The poor old savages merely pursued animistic beliefs and practices. And so it went. All along the line of cultural traits, including material culture. Here the Europeans had cities and guns, armies and kings, money and bureaucrats, wigs and leather shoes, while the others struggled to make out, doing it tough without war and slaves, without firearms and prisons.

Gordon Childe and others such as Robert Braidwood and Robert Carneiro gave the following attributes of what they called civilization. That is, VBH societies. Urban centres (cities), metallurgy, writing, surplus, calendar, plough, wheeled cart, sailing ships, measurement, irrigation, specialised craftsmen, taxes, privileged ruling class, priestly class, central government, classes, monumental ceremonial centres. These are listed in Table 1.

Table 1. Attributes of early VBH societies.

#	attribute	status
1	Urban centres	
2	Monumental religious centres	Collapse with 1
3	Central government	Link to kingship
4	Classes	
5	Privileged ruling class	Collapse with 4
6	Priestly class	Collapse with 4
7	Specialised craftsmen	Present in HG societies
8	Surplus	Centrally concentrated; other kind before
9	Taxes	Centrally concentrated
10	Irrigation	Present in PNG Highlands
11	Plough	Collapse with 7
12	Wheeled cart	Collapse with 7
13	Metallurgy	Collapse with 7; comes later
14	Calendar	
15	Writing	Collapse with 14; comes later perhaps
16	Measurement	Collapse with 14
17	Sailing ships	Sailing vessels present in the Pacific and colonising Australia 40K yr BP

Table 1 also shows how many of these attributes can be thought of in the same category as others, thereby reducing the number of them. They can in fact be reduced to the following core list (Table 2).

Table 2. Shortlist of attributes of early VBH societies.

#	Attribute	Status
1	Urban centres	
2	King & court	Historically replaced by president etc.
3	Class	Cross culturally variable
4	Central surplus & taxes	
5	Army & war	Not all prosecute war
6	Literacy & numeracy	Perhaps later
7	Prostitution	My theory

Which leaves 5 key attributes that continue on and look unstoppable. But are they? If at 5 million years into human evolution a snapshot had been taken of the then present and acknowledgement made to the past record, nobody in their right mind would have bet against any version of DMP society being unstoppable, continuing forever, or as long as human life survived. But look what happened there.

Proposed causes

I turn now to causes and explanations that have been proposed to account for the drama after the Ice. It has been suggested that in regard to the onset of VBH societies there is "no single, powerful, comprehensive explanation of the past" (Wenke 1999:693). This echoes older conclusions of similar bent: "No one major innovation caused civilization" (Fagan 1977:260). So we are offered various conjectures, hypotheses, theories if you will, for the origins of VBH societies. These range across causal factors such as climate change, agricultural intensification, large-scale irrigation schemes, population growth, warfare and territorial circumscription, and structural (social) factors. However, it is worth noting at the outset that "in contemporary archaeology there is a widespread sense that the key points of analysis in understanding the origins of early states must be at a socioeconomic and political level, not just demographic, physical environments, and the assumption of warfare" (Wenke 1999:360). Wenke (1999) devotes summaries in eight chapters of data from all over the VBH world to show that not only is climate change an inadequate causal hypothesis, but so are technology, economy and demography. As all but socio-political causation have well and truly fallen out of favour with modern archaeological thinking, I will quickly skip over most of these, merely mentioning them along with words of contemporary rejection or qualification of them.

(i) Climate change

Lewis Binford (1968) called these changes post-Pleistocene adaptations. The end of the Pleistocene saw the end of the Ice Ages, with global climate ameliorating, glaciers retreating, land bridges between continents (Asia and North America) and continents and islands (New Guinea, Tasmania, Australia) being flooded. The first place affected appears from the archaeological record to have been Southwest Asia. There, as already stated above, the strata yield the evidence of first agriculture as certain plant species (grasses) are harvested and their seeds sown for further harvest, certain species of animals formerly hunted, now beginning to be brought under the control of herders. These early agricultural societies give a suite of evidence for the management and control of crops and stock, the institution of granaries, of the first towns and cities, so-called because of their size outstripping in population and area that of villages. And even more dramatically, we witness the first fortifications.

During the last interglacial, some 120,000 years ago, the world's climate was approximately as warm as today. This lasted for a period of about 10,000 years. The planet was similar to today in terms of land size and shape, the seas, and vegetation (Gowlett 1984:96). In that favourable period, Gowlett (1984:96) continues, humans probably spread further than ever before, but the general course of events was vastly different from the Recent 10,000 years. There was no agriculture, no sudden development towards "civilization," and "no higher technology" (Gowlett 1984:96). Although the environment back then offered the same kind of opportunities as did the Holocene, those opportunities *"were not taken in the same way"* (Gowlett 1984:96, emphasis mine).

This clearly shows that any postulated causal arrow that goes climate change → agriculture → VBH societies, must be rejected. Such climatic and environmental conditions did not, and therefore do not necessarily lead to the Recent developments. Instead we have to ask: this time it happened, why not back then? Or perhaps more pertinently, it didn't happen last time when conditions were like this, why did it happen this time? Gowlett (1984:148) makes this telling comment:

> Although the Holocene changes may have provided a stimulus for human development we may suspect that something similar would have happened anyway. Evolutionary change had been so rapid from 30,000 to 10,000 years ago that a further 10,000 years would probably have brought enormous development whatever the climate.

It seems clear that climatic and environmental factors cannot be linked to direct causality in the events of the drama occurring after the Ice.

(ii) Agricultural intensification

Grinding stones are reported archaeologically from Egypt, to have suddenly appeared at 15,000 years ago. They have been linked to cereal and tuber processing (Gowlett 1984:152). However, the first signs of plant and animal domestication appear some 12,000 to 10,000 years ago (Gowlett 1984:156). Even then it is not easy to find firm evidence, but by 7000 years ago farming villages, cultivated crops and domesticated animals are evident over large areas of the Old World, while similar developments were beginning in the Americas (Gowlett 1984:156). The changes did not happen overnight as it were, but compared to 6 million years of hominid hunting and gathering, the "greatest ever alteration of economy came amazingly suddenly" (Gowlett 1984:156).

In Southeast Asia yams were domesticated 9,000 years ago, while in China the use of rice dates to least 7,000 years ago (Gowlett 1984:166).

Gowlett (1984:172) claims two essential elements of civilization were food production and "modern man, with the brain to organize." White (2007:355-356) agreed, claiming that the development of agriculture, "the harnessing of solar energy in the form of plants and animals ... produced civilization." There certainly appears to be a correlation of agricultural intensification with VBH developments. However Wenke (1999:428) concludes that agricultural intensification "seems to have been more a result than a cause of the emergence of complex societies."

(iii) Irrigation agriculture

Between the DMP and irrigation agriculture we must see a set of decisions: why irrigation is necessary or better, who is going to irrigate, how is it going to be done, what volume of productivity is the goal, what volume of water is needed, who is going to draw up a plan, who is going to dig carry and labour? These are human decisions; social actions taken by social actors.

Wenke's (1999:424) "review of the evidence from Southwest Asia suggests that irrigation cannot be said to be the 'primary cause' of early

Southwest Asian cultural complexity." In fact all core attributes of VBH societies appear in the archaeological record before irrigation systems.

He thus concludes: "the premise that irrigation systems ... are primary determinants of cultural evolution [is] ... for the most part, rejected" (Wenke 1999:636).

(iv) Population growth

We have already agreed with Wenke (1999) above to reject demographic factors in causality. But let us consider it further very briefly here. Again, social actors are required between the DMP population level and the VBH population level, to decide why a larger population is necessary or better, what DMP population control constraints are to be lifted.

Wenke (1999:426) argues that "if one graphs the approximate population of Greater Mesopotamia from about 8000 BC [10,000 BP] to about 3000 BC [5000 BP] against evidence of activity specialization, monumental architecture, agricultural productivity, and other indications of cultural complexity, then an impressively close correlation is apparent. However, he also quotes Robert McC. Adams: "population increases generally followed ... Urban Revolution ... [there is] simply no evidence for gradual population increases that might have helped to precipitate the Urban Revolution" (Wenke 1999:427). Gowlett (1984:172) too, says food production "made high population density inevitable – but that could only work if the human society was organized." Concentration of population, social organization, and "social hierarchy" all played a part (Gowlett 1984:174).

(v) Warfare & environmental circumscription

This is the inverse of the above; with population density the variable of interest now, rather than absolute levels, enforced by territorial size being reduced and military threats on the new reduced borders. Again, who makes the decisions: why not just give in to the threat from neighbours, why fight, how to fight, what's the plan, who will build walls, how to design them, labour, what weapons can be invented, do we need a higher level of social organisation, what sort of structure, who leads that?

Despite the "massive fortifications" at Jericho showing that "fears of attack were real 9,000 years ago" (Gowlett 1984:160) - the wall is 3m thick and several metres high, with an impressive stone tower built into it (Gowlett 1984:161), Wenke (1999:427) is able to claim that the importance of warfare at the beginning of VBH societies is not "manifestly evident" (Wenke 1999:427), at least universally. On the southern Mesopotamian plains, for example, walling of towns only becomes common "some centuries" after urbanism (Wenke 1999:427).

From the Late Palaeolithic cemetery at Jebel Sahaba, excavated during the Aswan Dam project in Egypt, 58 human skeletons were recovered. Almost half of these people, men, women and children, died violently. Flint flakes were found embedded in bones, neck vertebra, pelvic girdles, and elsewhere. Savage cut marks occurred on the bones of some. The excavators point out that this level of violence could not be sustained for long (Gowlett 1984:153). Wendorf, one of the excavators, suggested that climatic conditions were deteriorating at this time, possibly leading to increased conflicts between groups competing for scarce resources (Gowlett 1984:153). But there is no way of testing this proposed link between climate, resource circumscription and warfare.

However, we can check whether fortifications and evidence for warfare are universal at this time. They are not. In the Indus, for example, only 3 of 463 known sites from this crucial formative period have walls (Wenke 1999:493). And with regard to China, warfare can be dismissed as simply another "expression of more fundamental changes going on" (Wenke 1999:532).

(vi) Structural factors of an individual or social kind

So we come to the acceptable explanation of modern times. Contemporary archaeologists are "trying to see" this era as populated with "individuals, real, live people" (Wenke 1999:409). This has led to many arguments which suggest we must look with more scrutiny at what became the higher levels of social, economic and political life (Wenke 1999:374). Hand in hand with this goes the "ideology that legitimized the strict hierarchies of power, prestige, and wealth, and the social relationships among the many peoples in these hierarchies are a crucial focus of analysis" (Wenke 1999:429).

"What factors stimulate the production of surpluses and thus create the conditions for the establishment of social classes and administrative hierarchies?" (Wenke 1999:424). As I quoted above, VBH developments "could only work if the human society was organized" (Gowlett 1984:172). Concentration of population, social organization, and "social hierarchy" all played a part (Gowlett 1984:174). "Economic exploitation joins tyranny and so states are born" (Wenke 1999:362). KC Chang for China agreed that wealth "was itself the product of concentrated political power" (Wenke 1999:533).

Early Mesopotamian records show a yearning for the past, a past without VBH attributes, when all people were of equal worth, no-one had power over others (Wenke 1999:338). It appears the masses – at least as recorded here for some societies at some times - did not join in these new developments willingly. Or if they did, initially, the outcomes were not in the end the kinds of consequences they had foreseen and desired.

So how did it happen? The discussion of change or intensification then centres on key social and political players recorded for various of these DMP societies, figures known variously as chiefs, Divine Chiefs, Potlatch Chiefs, Big Men, etc. For ease of readers' confrontations with terminology, I will refer to all of them as variants on Big Men (BM). I then build on the statistical argument used in chapter 3, to show how we can characterise what might have happened if BM drove the onset of VBH societies (by marshalling surpluses but refusing to redistribute them as happened in the past).

Intensification in the DMP

Let us return now to historical ethnography to see what DMP societies, as recorded my modern anthropologists, might tell us about the transition from such societies into something else. What steps are taken and by whom? How does it work? Again Sahlins (1974) will be my major source, though there will be others too.

First, a statement from Sahlins (1974:87) to set us in context. The

> three elements of the DMP so far identified – small labor
> force differentiated essentially by sex, simple technology,
> and finite production objectives – are systematically
> interrelated. Not only is each in reciprocal bond with the
> others, but each by its own modesty of scale is adapted
> to the nature of the others. Let any one of these elements
> show an unusual inclination to develop, it meets from the
> others the increasing resistance of an incompatibility. The

normal systematic resolution of this tension is restoration
of the status quo ('negative feedback'). Only in the event
of an historic conjuncture of additional and external
contradictions ('overdetermination') would the crisis pass
over into destruction and transformation.

Thus do we witness six million years of DMP social organisation. These
are societies conservative in the limit, while paradoxically being culturally
dynamic, determined to retain what is was they possessed, something
one might romantically regard as a quality of life never known by man
or woman since. Negative feedback was their great ally. Additional and
external contradictions their enemies and seeds of destruction. And it
is these that begin in ever so small steps to intensification, where the
"success of only a few" becomes an "invitation to violence" (Sahlins
1974:88).

Kinship, chieftanship and even the ritual order emerge as economic forces
(Sahlins 1974:101). Such that a kinship system like Hawaiian can be seen
to be a more intensive economic system than Eskimo, for the former
has a greater degree of classification, a more extensive identification of
collateral and lineal relatives. This can be generalised beyond kinship
terms to include all "status terms" (Service 1971). All else equal then,
a kinship system like Hawaiian will generate a greater tendency to
surplus than will Eskimo (Sahlins 1974:23). So the intensification is
potentially well and truly embedded in the social structure, and we can
see it expressed roughly quantitatively through status terms.

Quoting from Firth's account of a famine on Tikopia during 1952-54,
he notes that while the society "managed a kind of moral continuity it
showed itself founded on a basic discontinuity." A kind of "atomization"
occurred; economic decomposition set in on several fronts, most notably

in property and distribution; the solidarity of the elementary family was revealed; land formerly held in common became a cause of contention; there was a decrease in sharing, an increase in theft; manners continued as morals degenerated; households became fortresses of self-interest; "social drawbridges" came up; sallies against the gardens of kith and kin went forth. The Tikopian polity "had begun to unhinge" (all quotes from Sahlins 1974:143).

Then it happens. As the structure is politicised, especially as it is centralised in ruling chiefs, the household economy is mobilised in a larger cause (Sahlins 1974:130). For political life is a "stimulus to production" (Sahlins 1974:135). For example, the systems of status competition found in Melanesia develop economic impact from the "ambition of aspiring big-men" (Sahlins 1974:135). Leadership "generates domestic surplus" (Sahlins 1974:140).

All this while keeping in mind the maxim: "men do not personally construct their power over others; they come to power. Power resides in the office, in an organized acquiescence to chiefly privileges and organized means of upholding them" (Sahlins 1974:139). But the DMP chief's power is tied to redistribution. If he hoards and exploits, he loses support of the people (Wenke 1999:358, citing David Webster). But this was about to change.

Marvin Harris (1979) identifies Big Men as nodes to intensify production. The crucial step for Harris is the rise of chiefdoms, which he links to the appearance of the BM. Influential older men whose advice and guidance the community seeks and follows, are found at the centre of events. They not only intensify production (through urging, cajoling, brow-beating, pleading), they also carry out redistribution of centrally collected goods, and lead the way in fighting and trading. They will come to an office the society is now willing to have established.

But after a long pedigree of DMP redistribution, more and more of the centrally collected surplus remains with the BM, as he begins to alter the balance between redistribution and appropriation. So before, in the DMP, where we saw a uniform distribution of wealth, this is now being replaced by the rapidly changing social structures in which the BM garners it all, redistributing less than all, then only a fraction. Before we know it, the BM has become a Rogue Individual, a BM gone mad – mad in the sense of overthrowing a history of tradition, morality and political behaviour, against all apparent DMP logic. Of course he can only do this if he can convince followers that his is the true way forward, that the office he now wishes to occupy is necessary for social success, that the new symbols incorporated must replace the old irrelevant ones to bring benefits to everybody.

The RI appropriates, with support from followers if need be, and force where necessary. Beyond his court, he now sees no need to redistribute. These are the new rules, within a new social structure, which have to quickly be made into laws and embedded in new approving – or at least fate accepting - belief systems. The new frequency distribution of wealth across the transitioning society is a geometric series. After the RI takes his slice, his princelings follow with theirs, the new generals with theirs, and so it goes. Most people now merely get bad news.

So the key to understanding this transition, this transformation, is the BM gone mad, become an RI. Note however, that it is not my intention to throw babies out with bathwaters. For a famine did occur on Tikopia, wheat and barley, and later rice and corn, did attain wide distribution in appropriate environments, with a consequent capacity for larger and larger surpluses, population did begin to grow more rapidly in some of these areas, and some RIs no doubt had to hurriedly build fortifications to keep at bay those who did not approve of the new appropriations, the new rules and laws, the new thugs in charge. Having said that, let me examine the transformation with a focus on the RI, and consider such a phenomenon somewhat abstractly – yes, mathematically - to see what theory we can develop around this.

Linear transformations

If we think back to the previous chapter, we recall the probability density functions for wealth distribution in two different social forms given by equations (3.3) and (3.4). As society changes from a very egalitarian hunting and gathering DMP type social form to a VBH type, the distribution of wealth becomes less evenly spread and more clumped to certain individuals at one end of the distribution. This is a transformation, a certain kind of change over time. In mathematics, a transformation is an operation in which one set of elements is transformed into another set of elements (Sterling 2009:148). Earlier I have referred to this outcome set as the VBH set.

Slightly more formally, for any two sets V and W, a transformation T from V into W associates with each $x \in V$ an element in W that we denote by *Tx* (Schneider & Barker 1973:211). In other words a transformation can be thought of as a different form of our old friend the function.

In chapter 3 I also introduced matrices and vectors. I will make further use of them here to talk theoretically about the origins of VBH societies. More specifically, I will be concerned with what are known as linear transformations. A linear transformation is a particular type of transformation in which one set of vectors is transformed into another vector set using what is called a linear operator.

If we call the transformation T, we can characterise it in terms of two vectors $\mathbf{v}_1$ and $\mathbf{v}_2$:

$$T: \mathbf{v}_1 \rightarrow \mathbf{v}_2$$

showing that our transformation transforms vector $\mathbf{v}_1$ into vector $\mathbf{v}_2$.

A linear operator is the rule governing the transformation; prescribing how it works. A linear operator can, and for our purposes here will, take matrix form. For example, if we have a vector $\mathbf{v}$ which we wish to transform through transformation $T(\mathbf{v})$, we can do so using the linear operator matrix A. First of all we write

$$\mathbf{v} = \begin{bmatrix} 1 \\ 4 \\ -2 \end{bmatrix}$$

say, and

$$T(\mathbf{v}) = T\left(\begin{bmatrix} 1 \\ 4 \\ -2 \end{bmatrix}\right).$$

Then we describe the transformation like this:

$$T(\mathbf{v}) = A\,\mathbf{v} \tag{4.1}$$

which reads: the transformation T on vector $\mathbf{v}$ is performed by multiplying vector $\mathbf{v}$ by the linear operator matrix A. By way of example, let us suppose we have a linear operator A of the form

$$A = \begin{bmatrix} 2 & 1 & 5 \\ -3 & 4 & 2 \\ 6 & -1 & -2 \end{bmatrix}$$

and we take the transformation of vector **v** as above:

$$\begin{bmatrix} 2 & 1 & 5 \\ -3 & 4 & 2 \\ 6 & -1 & -2 \end{bmatrix} \begin{bmatrix} 1 \\ 4 \\ -2 \end{bmatrix}.$$

This gives

$$A\mathbf{v} = \begin{bmatrix} 2+4-10 \\ -3+16-4 \\ 6-4-4 \end{bmatrix} = \begin{bmatrix} -4 \\ 9 \\ -2 \end{bmatrix}.$$

I have used integers here to keep the example as simple as possible. But of course in real life things get more complicated. Especially when I am seeking to define the VBH set which does not have integer elements but rather has the form {king, priest, accountant,...}. The equivalent of the vector **v** above will in turn constitute the DMP elements {hunter, gatherer, ...}. So where does that leave us with this theory of linear transformations and the linear operator?

Let's think about it in a more abstract form, where the linear operator

$$A = \begin{bmatrix} a_{11} & a_{12} & a_{13} \\ a_{21} & a_{22} & a_{23} \\ a_{31} & a_{32} & a_{33} \end{bmatrix}$$

is defined following its use in mathematical ecology as the so-called community matrix (May 1974:22) whose elements a_{ij} describe the effect of species j upon species i near equilibrium. What does all this mean?

It means we can assign to the elements of our linear operator certain values for how any one kind of entity (species) interacts with all other kinds (species). This of course also means that indulgence is begged in order to once again, as in chapter 2, entertain the notion that certain given social entities can be usefully thought of analogously as species. While this may at first take seem cumbersome, I suggest on the contrary, as I did for the use of species of sex workers earlier, that it allows an interpretation to emerge from the theory which gives social and cultural meaning to the linear transformation.

Which is to say I am suggesting that the theory can be interpreted – with that indulgence of a species analogy – as a linear operator which takes us from a DMP set to a VBH set, being made up of a set of elements whose values reflect the effects of one upon another. What sort of effects?

If we assume that any given DMP society might be made up of elements that look like {hunter, gatherer, shaman, big man, ...}, where the last term can be substituted for potlatch chief in a society of the NWC form (see chapter 3). Assume further that the interactions between kinds of roles in such a DMP society are the elements of the community matrix, such that we see the effects of say, a big man on a hunter, a big man on a gatherer, a big man on a yam digger, and so on.

In mathematical ecology the type of interaction sets the sign of the non-zero community matrix elements. The sign structure of such an m X m matrix depends on the effect of species j on species i as being positive (+), neutral (0), or negative (-). May's (1974:25) description of this setup leads to a set of effects of species j on species i versus the effect of species i on species j.

Six different categories of interaction emerge. They are in fair agreement with how human ecologists see the interactions between human populations as essentially: predation, competition, cooperation and mutualism (Hardesty 1971:160). Most of the six are of the form 00, ++, 0+, 0-, in which we see situations where any influence one species exerts has either no effect or a mutually positive effect on the other. In other words not much happens. The DMP goes on unabated. However, the other two categories are -- and +-. The former in ecology constitutes competition and I think we can interpret it the same way here in the social situation. Perhaps the outcome of two or more Big Men jockeying for prestige and cultural gain.

The latter is ecologically a predator-prey interaction (predation) and emerges as the most interesting and significant interaction for my present purposes. I interpret this as a big man or potlatch chief gone mad. Which is to say such accumulators suddenly defy the logic of their culture and history, throw precedent to the wind, and take to refusing, unlike generations of their ancestors and a whole world of their DMP chiefly compatriots, to give back what they have accumulated. Surplus for the first time in human history is appropriated. Kept and hoarded, filling the coffers of this new social type in ways previously only dreamed about.

The key elements of this community matrix, as linear operators, change the entire spectrum of politics and economics in these cultures while transitioning away from DMP rules and regulations. It is in the linear transformations that we are able to see key elements of linear operators – some predatory social type preying on others (for goods, funds, capital), while at the same time coming to embody the collective - in achieving these dramatic empirical changes.

And just what do these Big Men gone mad become? A species emergent and unique. I interpret them as Rogue Individuals (RIs). Essentially, these are Big Men morphing into surplus possessing controllers of wealth, of land, of cultural beliefs, of groups of supporters who quickly form religions, ethnic identities and armies. Then ultimately, they attain control of the entire society. The theory (chapter 3) defines the existence of a set of unique attributes called the VBH set. And in turn, the VBH set is seen to be uniquely brought about by the political actions of BM becoming RIs.

Rogue Individuals

Recall again the above: I propose a linear transform to move from the old vector set of the DMP to the new vector set of VBH. This creates, as it were, the VBH set. That's where it comes from. Where its elements come from. And what creates it? The linear operator A. That is, from equation (4.1) above:

$$T(\mathbf{v}) = A\,\mathbf{v}$$

where $\mathbf{v}$ is the vector set from above, T marks the transformation, and A is the linear operator (some of whose elements can be interpreted as representing Rogue Individuals). In the final washup the transformation yields the outcomes for the scheme of VBH social change. We can think about such a scheme as the following:

Big Man $\rightarrow$ Rogue Individual $\rightarrow$ King.

Having seen above how hierarchy may affect energy harnessed, my question for the next section of the theory is how does the RI affect hierarchy? Sahlins (2000a:25) supplies the bounds within which the answer lies: agency occurs "not in distinction to structure, but in certain relations to it." For the RI is the mechanism, I suggest, that allows this to happen, that (or is it who?) makes it happen. The fuzzy operations of means of production or techno-environmental factors just happening to cause energy to be harnessed and utilised in certain ways are thus replaceable by the actions of real human actors as political and power broking figures. As a key element of the VBH set, my central thesis is that the RI becoming king provides a pivotal causative actor in the development of VBH societies, one who comes to embody the social and its collective powers. This however, is not just a mindless variation of the great man in history theme. Nor is it the Hobbes to Foucault monster devil that Sahlins (2000b) warned us about (the "recurrent attempt to make individual need and greed the basis of sociability, p.533; where "self-interest is the nature of the individual, power is the essence of the social", p.549). It links seamlessly to a mode of production and a means of production – with clear origins in the DMP - in which the RI is a central node of organisation, of management, and even of ideas. He and his kitchen cabinet of follower supporters become the engine room of the new social dynamics and symbolism. And of course it links also to those means, the tools and skills, the plants and animals available for cropping and herding, the irrigation which is put in place, all creating the surplus which the RI will appropriate centrally and deploy to his political ends. Let me give some examples.

The great American anthropologist Franz Boas (1960) talks about how an individual, if strong enough, and if followers are willing, can bring about rapid social and cultural change. Rogue Individuals bring their allies and followers along on the journey to power. For priests too can be agents for rapid change due to their own ambitions, even though they are generally thought of as the keepers of so-called conservative traditions (Boas 1960:160). "Changes are facilitated in all of those cases in which customs are entrusted to the care of a few individuals" (Boas 1960:160), the RI and his gang, his group, his faction.

Especially is this so when conditions suit. Which is to say, when there is instability, or rapidly altering hierarchical relations. A power seeking group may impose itself by force, bringing cultural change. For only "when a new culture ... is imposed by force ... may one group succeed in the attempt to impose radical changes in culture" (Boas 1960:163). When there are foreign ideas or violent changes owing to disturbance "the opportunity [is] given to the individual to establish new lines of thought that may give a new direction to cultural change" (Boas 1960:163-4).

Stratification (i.e. hierarchy) is also seen as important. For lack of stratification may account for "the intense conservatism" of cultures studied by Boas, such as the late nineteenth century early twentieth century Eskimo (Boas 1960:159). (Though of course such "conservatism" in cultures like Eskimo has been hotly critiqued in modern times (e.g. Sahlins 2000c), and shown to be quite something else.)

The historian Arnold Toynbee "proposed that new civilizations arise out of a creative surge, expressed most strongly perhaps in certain individuals" (Bohm & Peat 1987:204-5). As with disturbance, instability, or even rapidly rising hierarchy, the creative surge emerges as a "response to some kind of challenge" (Bohm & Peat 1987:207).

Important insights on the RI or equivalent emerge from a modern political study of corruption and democracy in Thailand (Pasuk & Sungsidh 1994). Highly relevant to the theory, these data provide analogy about rogue individuals of a modern kind, corrupt, criminal, and powerful. The study also provides background on power, its acquisition and maintenance, as well as wealth accumulation in patron client networks which often involve corruption.

Interestingly they also refer to these players as big men or big people. The first thing they must do is establish a group of followers. In Thai culture this ensures a flow of gifts and favours to the big man. He in return, sends similar back, creating and maintaining their loyalty. He is thus able to see off competition from other would be big men and their factions. This is expensive for a big man, who must then seek to recoup expenditure. The source of this is public funds; corruption is instituted (Pasuk & Sungsidh 1994:5).

Such corruption has long been entrenched in Thai culture. It extended all the way from the king to the village. Big men who began to accrue wealth and power were incorporated by the king as a network upon which official titles would be bestowed. Tribute payments came back to the king, and worked their way down the network. Diversions of public monies paid for it all; the higher the office the larger the diversion of funds would be (Pasuk & Sungsidh 1994:7).

Because much of this activity involves acting outside the law, big men need protection. Police, military, public officials all play their part, for remuneration of course. As salaries are mostly low, augmentation of this kind is eagerly sought. Old chums are willing to help, then gratefully accept the kickbacks. Much of the money comes from things like protection rackets: the rich get richer and the poor get problems.

Pasuk & Sungsidh (1994:19) discuss political theories relating to the development of democratic institutions in new states where the concentration of economic, social and political power lead to corruption as the powerful work to maintain and grow their power. Authors they cite argue that the modernization process goes hand in glove with corruption. It was true for the eighteenth century United Kingdom, for the nineteenth century United States, and so it is for countries such as traditional and modern Thailand. This leads to an inference: thus was it true for early Mesopotamia and other VBH societies of the Holocene. In many pre-modern societies patronage, favouritism and the appropriation of public funds for personal use were acceptable and legitimate forms of behaviour. The distinction between the king's purse and the public coffers was blurred. During and after the transition to modern institutions of bureaucracy and parliament, these traditional practices persisted.

Pasuk & Sungsidh (1994:19)

So while early VBH societies had no parliaments, they did have bureaucracies. These, along with their leaders, oversaw patronage, favouritism and appropriation of surpluses then public funds. Secondly, those same political theorists suggest, in any period of transition many people become confused over issues of public and private domains, giving opportunities for those who would to get away with corrupt behaviour. Remember, the RI cum king was also instituting law (recall Hanumurabi and his law code in Babylon, introduced about 5790 BP.) This corrupt new wealth literally buys legitimacy. And though the state apparatus and its bureaucracy expand and gain greater control, as force becomes legalised, such controls can lead again to further corruption. Finally they suggest a link between corruption and instability (Pasuk & Sungsidh 1994:20), as those who have missed out complain, protest, have to be subdued, seek alliances elsewhere.

One could easily argue that similar practices occurred in VBH societies of the Recent period. Hence my chosen name for the phenomenon Rogue Individuals, takes on another meaning. He is not only rogue for being the Big Man gone mad; he is corrupt, and his corruption expands and grows as his power and ambition scale the heights of social domination. Then there arises a network of corruption, grown from patron client relations, with a correlation of corruption with social and structural closeness to the RI cum king. The RI's cronies are in it with him, up to their ears, and as the fry get smaller further (socially) away, so the need for large graft drops off. We end up at the very bottom stratum of society where serfs, slaves and landless peasants get not much more than bad news.

Support for the RI interpretation also comes from early documents on ancient VBH societies. Lewthwaite is cited for claiming that in such circumstances "the motor for social change is the ambition of certain individuals to dominate and control their fellow human beings" (Wenke 1999:547). Gowlett (1984:149) speculates that "there were probably individuals who saw what was necessary before it became imperative, and who could attempt to lead the way."

In Mesopotamia for example, Sargon of Akkad is reported to have risen to power about 4350 BP. This event was of such moment it meant "the political fabric of ancient Southwest Asia was forever changed" (Wenke 1999:420). From 4000 BP to 3800 BP Greater Mesopotamia fragmented, as various kings "established contending states" (Wenke 1999:422). But out of this instability and disturbance, by 3792 BP Hanumurabi had established the Babylonian empire. As I noted earlier, the "many documents of his reign ... reflect a skilful politician" (Wenke 1999:423). Speaking of Babylon, in 332 BC (i.e. about 2332 BP) the incomparable Alexander marched into Egypt and "built the city of Alexandria" (Wenke 1999:461).

In Egypt Menes/Narmer, "a minor official from Upper Egypt, rose to power and conquered Lower Egypt at about 3100 BC" [5100 BP] (Wenke 1999:448). He and his successors built a "theocratic political system over the entire navigable length of the Egyptian Nile" (Wenke 1999:448). They built a capital at Memphis. Then major construction projects were undertaken in the centuries before 2700 BC [4700 BP]. In Egypt not only such constructions, but economic exchange generally was controlled almost entirely through the king (Wenke 1999:449), whether that was Narmer, his successors, Alexander, or others. In addition, services were delivered in the name of the king. (Note: not in the name of energy harnessed.)

A stele set up by Ur-Nammu, king of Ur, in about 2100 BC [4100 BP] symbolizes the authority of the king being drawn from the god. There is also an Ur-Nammu law code which begins:

> Then did Ur-Nammu, the mighty man, the king of Ur, the
> king of Sumer and Akkad, ... establish justice in the land,
> and by force of arms did he turn back evil and violence.

> Gowlett (1984:8-9)

The ancient Maya of Meso America "all shared in the material wealth that the king provided the community through successful performance of his powers" (Wenke 1999:587). Tellingly, he "invented ideas that harnessed social energy" (Wenke 1999:587).

At times the RI operated surrounded by followers, and group members who constituted the new elites. In the Valley of Mexico "an important factor ... was the imposition of tributes by elites" (Wenke 1999:576). For Oaxaca, as reported by Kowalewski & Feinstein: with "changing functions and degrees of chiefly or state power ... predilections of elites changed" (Wenke 1999:584). In the Mississippi Valley of North America (Wenke 1999:668) "elite groups manage to appropriate a society's resources and manage to perpetuate their domination". This saw the social structure come to include a "redistributor-chief", quite possibly something very akin to a Big Man or Potlatch Chief, going mad and changing towards a RI, leading his elite to new power and wealth.

So what can we conclude about the RI? What does all this anthropology, history, archaeology, ancient history, and modern political analysis tell us?

It suggests the RI and his followers, his trusty band, become the first elites. They usurp control of the surplus or a large part of it. They take over this wealth which in DMP terms we would see quite legitimately as public funds (i.e. for equitable distribution by former redistributive Big Men and Chiefs of one kind or another). They blur the distinction between this new public wealth and their fast growing private wealth. The new wealth is streamed into a power source as police and military are established alongside a bureaucracy and legal system. The first professional merchant class is formed, for systematic state-sponsored exploitation of the masses.

And in addition, one group of cronies is given charge of the new belief system, raising the king to divine status in some cases, to inalienable rapture in all cases, ensuring conformity of belief and ritual as it is laid down by this new class of priests. Their job it is to ensure the people at large kowtow, behave, adopt the new desired morality, and pay due homage (as well as taxes).

The RI is above all a skilled politician. Among other things he and his band institute a theocratic political system with him at the head. From there he and his follower advisers can design and create empires, energy harnessing schemes, encourage development of and funding for new technologies, build cities and fortify them against potential or real challenges, establish roads and expand trade communications, all the while building wealth relentlessly. His exchange is commercial, originating in formerly intertribal trade, but now rendered appropriate for his intrasocietal ends (White 2007:334).

The Big Man gone mad becomes corruption personified. Taking on the commercial values of VBH society, as opposed to the intrasocietal exchange that prevailed in DMP societies, where a context of kinship, hospitality and friendship prevailed, he adopts the "natural and normal features" of the commercial process: "[l]ying, cheating, misrepresentation, and stealing" (White 2007:346-347). In former DMP societies changing almost too rapidly for most people to understand what is happening, there is disturbance, uncertainty and instability. Before the majority know it (metaphorically), they have had their rights taken away, along with their lands and livelihoods. They are suddenly the new serfs, peasants and slaves. Poor and or attractive women and boys are disposed to become another new VBH phenomenon: prostitutes. And temple brothels are built to house them.

From this central part of the theory, and especially from key insights provided by Pasuk & Sungsidh (1994), a prediction emerges which may possibly be testable by ancient historical or archaeological data. It concerns the building of monumental architecture, which essentially all VBH societies experienced quite quickly in their developmental histories. This is almost universally seen by archaeologists as waste. But it has been explained, or should I say given the functionalist interpretation, as picking up the economic slack in a system, giving idle hands something to do in times of unemployment, even if burning up valuable social wealth on wasteful extravagance. As Wenke (1999:547) said, perhaps these great wastes of energy and resources "stabilized these societies by reducing population growth and economic expansion."

Pasuk & Sungsidh (1994) show that corrupt big men in modern Thailand engaged in large scale construction projects (mostly roads, buildings, townships, but also sometimes temples) for two reasons. Firstly, such projects allowed and approved by the big men, gave opportunity for the big man's palm to be greased and his pockets lined by contractors. Cuts and kickbacks became standard behaviour (Pasuk & Sungsidh 1994:52-53).

This is possibly not as relevant for early VBH times as it is unlikely any private contracting existed back then. More probable, all construction was already under the control of the king and his cronies. Organisations that we could later see as state owned enterprises. So kickbacks were probably less relevant. Also, we have to remember, that in this early phase of VBH societies, there was no money, even though there was use value of certain commodities. Exchange was still mostly in kind, of goods being given back and forth (Wenke 1999:419). So it is hard to see how an RI would benefit from hiving off materials from his own projects. However, this is not to say that someone down the food chain a little did not benefit: perhaps a trusted follower supporter, given oversight of such a project, hiving off materials to build his own temple somewhere else.

However, secondly, the big man has to appear concerned with the status and welfare of his community (Pasuk & Sungsidh 1994:86). He must be seen as an upstanding supporter of community values and religion. He donates to temples, builds new ones, finances ceremonies and pilgrimages, constructs these huge monuments. Now we're possibly on to something. This second finding allows us to move beyond the functionalist interpretations (of monumental construction being useful to take up slack in the economy) and predict: that large scale monumental architecture in early VBH societies will be accompanied by revelations of the glory and greatness of the generous funding benefactor, the king, along with the perceived advantages these new monuments brought to the society and community.

Collapse

> Wars, conquests, and imperialism marked the development of the great cultures of the Agricultural Revolution. International competition and conflict became intensified as cultures developed within the rather fixed and finite limits of natural resources. Continued and repeated destruction as a concomitant of chronic warfare, and the ruthless exploitation of conquered lands through slavery, tribute, and taxation, eventually brought about the decline and downfall of one nation and empire after another.
>
> White (2007:352)

Archaeologists and ancient historians tend to see VBH societies attaining full-blown status with the beginnings of writing, making for a several thousand year buildup of the phenomenon since the first archaeological indicators such as towns and cities appeared. During the course of their histories, "many have risen and fallen" (Gowlett 1984:194). These "enclaves of order" were "vulnerable to outside people who had no cause to respect their stability" (Gowlett 1984:194). In fact, these systems were "not suited to stability" (White 2007:353). Hence they could easily break down. Invasion, famine or disease could easily and soon upset the balance, ensuring societal collapse.

In this section I will show very briefly that in linear operators of the form discussed above as community matrices, there is built into these matrices a tendency to reveal population fluctuations which are highly unstable. The new system, the becoming-VBH system, I will consider as that given by the equation (4.1), which is to say the linear operator and its outcome together make up the system.

However, I choose to keep this section mostly non-mathematical, as to lay down and explain the equations would virtually require copying a score or more of pages of quite difficult text verbatim. I suggest instead, that readers who desire to confront the technical details see May (1974).

May (1974:21-23) says of the community matrix that it not only summarizes the interactions between species, but it sets what he calls the neighbourhood stability. The temporal behaviour of such a system is given by what are known as the eigenvalues of the community matrix. Eigenvalues need not concern us too much here, but a simple way to think of them is as factors of vectors. For example if we have a vector

$$\mathbf{V} = \begin{bmatrix} 2 \\ 3 \end{bmatrix}$$

and we take a vector transform

$$T : \mathbf{V} \rightarrow \mathbf{V}^1$$

such that vector $\mathbf{V}$ is transformed into vector $\mathbf{V}^1$, where the latter is given by

$$\mathbf{V}^1 = \begin{bmatrix} 4 \\ 6 \end{bmatrix}$$

then we see clearly that the transform has involved multiplying the elements of $\mathbf{V}$ by 2. We then refer to the factor 2 as the eigenvalue of the vector.

This is a simple example involving a real number. However in general for the setup under discussion the eigenvalues of the community matrix are complex numbers (recall: these are numbers of the form $z = x + iy$). Then if any one eigenvalue has a positive real part (i.e. $x > 0$), there is an exponential factor (e.g. in May's equation 2.14, May 1974:22) which will grow ever larger over time, rendering any equilibrium unstable.

In regard to the m X m matrix which we have discussed as the community matrix, any disturbances from equilibrium most often lead to instability (May 1974:48). One of May's main points is that mathematical models of the kind he presents, with many species (i.e. in my case Big Men gone mad, generals, priests, donor hunters, donor gatherers,…) are in general less stable than models with few species (i.e. of the DMP type: hunter, gatherer,…). Obviously then, as such a matrix grows larger in the number of species (king, queen, prince, harem, concubines, priest,…) it becomes less and less stable.

May (1974:68-69) quotes and cites Richard Levins to the effect that a "number of quite independent lines of argument converge toward the assertion that there is often a limit to the complexity of systems." Too many "strong links" (king becoming more powerful, richer, general more powerful, … exploiting masses) will lead a system to almost certain instability.

May (1974:74) echoes the theme: in general mathematical models of this form, "increased complexity makes for diminished stability." In the theory I have chosen to characterise the onset of VBH societies via Big Men developing into Rogue Individuals then into Kings, the mathematics that accounts well for such a transformation also has built into it this outcome that the ultimate result for the system will be instability, or "increasing fragility" as Scheffer (2009:6) called it. The obvious prediction is one of ultimate system collapse.

The theory is unfortunately silent on time scales and the exact knowledge of which systems will collapse when. For example it applies well to all the early states of Mesopotamia and Southwest Asia, through to the Roman Empire, certain states in Meso America such as the Maya (though for many of these ancient states we remain uncertain as to the role of exogenous factors such as marauding hordes, invaders, etc.), but does not apply well to many modern states. However, that said, in modern times we have witnessed the collapse of the European colonial empires (British, French, Dutch, Spanish), of the former Soviet Union, many African states descending into genocide and chaos, the Balkans states, and in the present, Afghanistan. We also observe secession movements in Indonesia - East Timor successful and Aceh as yet unsuccessful, the southern Muslims in both Thailand and The Philippines, Bangladesh breaking away from Pakistan, Pakistan itself separating earlier from India, the Tamils in Sri Lanka, the Basques in Spain, itchings and rumblings in Wales and Scotland even. (Of course some of these were unions of colonial fiction, living through modern desires for political autonomy once again.) Differentiating these according to success or time scale may involve something to do with the above mentioned eigenvalues. I do not know. For how we ever calculate those from archaeology and ancient history, even recent history, is beyond me.

But whatever, one thing we can see – even if through a glass darkly - from my theoretical insights into origins of such complex systems as VBH societies, is their predicted collapse.

White's energy relation

Leslie White (e.g see 2007 [1959]) developed a theory of social evolution which, among many other things postulated a causal link between the amount of energy harnessed by any given society and the level of social development shown by that society. If E is energy harnessed, T is the efficiency with which that energy is utilised, and P the product, or goods and services produced, then

$$E \times T \to P. \tag{4.2}$$

That is, energy harnessed multiplied by the efficiency with which it is utilised, leads to product. Nowadays we would be more likely to write this in the form

$$P = f(E, T)$$

showing that P is a function of both E and T. White also used various other descriptors for P: social advancement, social evolution, cultural development, degree of development, progress. In his own formulation the law read (White 2007:55, italics in original): *"culture develops as the efficiency or economy of the means of controlling energy increases, other factors remaining constant."*

He also gave various breakdowns of this basic formula. One (White 2007:47, again italics in original) was

$$E(H \times N) \times T \to P$$

where he distinguished energy in terms of the human (H) and nonhuman (N) components. The human organism was for many peoples the only source of energy, bodily energy. Flowing water, winds, fire, agriculture, and so on, are some categories of nonhuman energy. So the above relation if we "hold the tool factor constant" leads to

$$H \times N \to P.$$

Another interpretation of the basic law (4.2) then became: *"culture advances as the proportion of nonhuman energy to human energy increases."*

Yet another variant is given as

$$E \times T \times V \rightarrow P$$

where V stands for environment. For it "is obvious", he says (White 2007:49), that every culture is determined by instrumental and environmental factors as well as by that of energy. In this case we see the product P as a function of three independent variables.

However in a case like this, "it is convenient and desirable to treat each one singly while disregarding the other two. In considering the culture process, we may think of any two of these factors as constants while we vary the third" (White 2007:49). Though he does not say so, this is the standard method for dealing with functions of two or more variables, using what are called partial derivatives (Simmons 1996:665-680) leading to partial differential equations (Farlow 1993): studying variation in one variable at a time, while holding the others constant. We won't follow him down that track however. (For having guided the way by mentioning it, he doesn't go down it either.)

Instead I will present one final variation on his social evolution formula. It is this:

$$T(Sb \times Pr \times D) \rightarrow society \; .$$

In this version the technological factor is "expressed in" the tools and processes of subsistence Sb, protection from the elements Pr, and defence from enemies D (White 2007:20). The product of these gives simply: society.

Now let me turn from the basic law and its variations to consider via a hypothetical example involving imagined societies, the extent to which the law or some of the variables involved, might be revealed in a simple empirical situation of technological, social and cultural change.

Let us imagine two societies which we will label S_1 and S_2 existing at a time t_0. The former consists of n individuals, men women and children, and is possessed of an iron age technology supplemented by some bronze tools, stone tools and wooden appliances. The latter consists of m individuals and is possessed of a similar technology. Let us call their technologies T_0. They are neighbouring societies who have some intermarriage and do some visiting. They speak different but mutually intelligible languages. Being iron age cultures both S_1 and S_2 are chiefdoms with big man chiefs C_1 and C_2 respectively. Both societies harness a level E_0 of energy. Each society has a level of wealth which we will call P_0.

Suppose that some individual or group of individuals in one of the societies, while carrying out other tasks, unearths a seam of coal, which they find attractive, play with, take as keepsakes, swap and trade, and eventually one or several of them drop into a fire. Coal's burning properties quickly become appreciated by both societies.

Further, let us assume that two brothers-in-law, b_1 from society S_1 and b_2 from S_2, are so impressed with coal burning, they decide to return to the exposed seam and bring a few sacks of it back to camp. Their tools are sufficient for the digging, the sacks their women sew, also. They make some impressive fires. Being inventive lads out for a lark, they begin to experiment with things put in the fires, so what happens to what. Leaves, wood, an old basket, all go the way of the flames. As does eventually, an iron pot. However w_1, a wife of b_1, on seeing this, wants to retrieve her pot, so first brings some water and pours it into the pot, thinking it will cool, not melt, and she can retrieve it.

But the water boils off, such is the heat of the fire. More water poured in, more boiled off. Then w_1 brings a lid and places it on the pot, to prevent the water boiling off. But the three people witness the lid being pushed up and down as the water vapour does its job. So-called steam power is observed.

Big discussions follow among members of both societies. Let there be a heavy lobby among members of S_1 to convince C_1 to literally keep a lid on this new fangled phenomenon. Let it go. People are happy with their DMP style underproduction, their leisure filled lifestyle, and see potential danger and fear attached to this new discovery.

Let there be a lobby among the members of S_2, or at least some of them, to C_2, to make something of this. Namely, a new way of iron smelting, by using a coal fired technique. Among the lobby group there is felt a need for a new social form to take care of the responsibility for this coal firing production, to design it, to facilitate it, to organize it, to manage it. It is suggested b_2 take on this head role, in charge of the operation. He accepts.

Now let us observe that at time $t_1 > t_0$ we see both societies working well, interacting as they did before, but with S_1 harnessing the amount of energy E_0 they have done for generations, maintaining P_0 level of wealth. While S_2 has escalated its energy harnessing by manufacturing vast amounts of new iron tools, some of which can be put to productive use, others for trade and sale to other societies. They are harnessing $E_2 > E_0$ amount of energy, and are now worth $P_2 > P_0$.

At time t_1, we then find S_1 with no coal fired iron smelting technology T_0 has P_0 while harnessing E_0; S_2 has a coal fired iron smelting technology (let's call it T_2), is vested of wealth P_2 while it harnesses E_2.

Imagine plotting a graph of P against E and T. We see immediate correlations: while E is low, T is low, P is low, yet when E is high, T is high, and P is high.

We could use these data to arrive at the White relation (4.2) which we wrote as

$$P = f(E,T).$$

This allows us to show that White's energy relation is not wrong, but rather was for its time highly insightful. However, for certain reasons, mostly to do with the modern notion of scientifically acceptable variables, we can try to do better by moving on from it. One reason, relating to the subjective, emotionally charged dependent variable P as social development or social advancement, or levels of same, of even as social progress, I have noted earlier. It is not, I stress again, just that in the late twentieth century as well as in this century we are being politically correct. That's not the issue. The issue is as I said earlier, and above, that none of these versions of the dependent variable has any genuine scientific validity.

Choosing his social evolution as a more scientifically sounding descriptor only goes some way to mollify things. For in the original it is constantly there as progress, higher levels of culture. P as goods and services might be one way to think about it validly; the products of social forces related to production (which perhaps carry a more intellectually satisfying connotation of links to mode of production, means of production, and even forces of production).

A second reason is that when we think about how energy harnessing comes about we run up against an issue I have raised already in relation to the role of the Rogue Individual in harnessing social alliances, appropriating redistributed goods and services, garnering a massive proportion of the surplus, driving social change (as a key element or elements within a linear operator community matrix in my theory of linear transformations). Energy harnessing comes about because some individual, some group, some class, some elite, somebody, demands, cajoles, pleads, decides, it be done. So that instead of energy E appearing as an independent variable in the final form of this analysis, as it does for White up to and including his relation (4.2), we need to view the place of harnessed energy as dependent upon just what is going on among members of society and the structures – both social and symbolic - developing or already in place. That is, energy will be some function of what we might term a set of state variables that determine the makeup of a society at any given time. This means

$$E = f(s_1, s_2, s_3, ... s_n) \tag{4.3}$$

for n state variables. Don't be confused; when I say state here I am not implying nation state or early city states. I mean that any social form whether it be the USA, France, ancient dynastic Egypt, the Aztecs, the Nuer, the Kwakiutl, the Aranda, the Maring, will have a set of state variables that describes its current state. When thinking of state variables that characterise a social system I am referring to population variables (size, growth rate), technological variables, political, economic, and other measures such as environmental (see Cowgill 1975, Hardesty 1977:193, where he quotes Cowgill). In regard to the political and economic I am therefore thinking of variables to do with social structure. So I need to say something about what is meant by social structure.

Radcliffe-Brown (1979:191-194) considered it to be about "persistent social groups" such as tribes, clans, nations, dyadic social relations between individuals, and differentiation by social role (individuals and groups, e.g. classes). If we think about these components of structure, what do we extract? Well, we see that both the second (dyadic relations) and third (social roles) would normally suggest notions of more or less seniority, respect, deference, and even more or less social power. That is, they connote hierarchy. And while the first is about grouping and identity (the classes discussed at length by White 2007), these groups too are hierarchical (lineage within clan within moiety within tribe or nation, for example).

Beattie (1964:60-63) emphasized the "formal, enduring aspects" of social institutions of interest, most probably reflecting Radcliffe-Brown's first point. Evans-Pritchard (1974) similarly: the enduring relationships that give social groups their identity and allow them to merge with and into larger entities (obviously with his Nilotic segmentary lineages in mind). Lienhardt (1966:156) argued that to be of practical use social structure needed to be broken down into "structures of relationship." This meant components such as political structure, family and kinship, economic, religious and so forth.

Levi-Strauss (1963:46) has this to say, using the avunculate's position in kinship as his example:

> to understand the avunculate we must treat it as one relationship within a system, while the system itself must be considered as a whole in order to grasp its structure. This structure rests upon four terms (brother,

> sister, father, and son), which are linked by two pairs of
> correlative oppositions in such a way that in each of the
> two generations there is always a positive relationship and
> a negative one ... This structure is the most elementary
> form of kinship that can exist. It is, properly speaking, *the*
> *unit of kinship.* [italics in original]

All up that's pretty woolly. But if we stick with Radcliffe-Brown's basic
notions, add in a movement towards Levi-Strauss' linked oppositions,
beef them up with a little formalism, I think a fairly clear picture may
emerge of social structure reflecting hierarchy. To this extent, following
the idea of Thom (1989:116), consider a structure S to consist of   levels
of sets of objects O_i such that at any given level $i = 2,3...n$, an object O_i
may be decomposed into objects O_{i-1} at level $i-1$.

For example, following Levi-Strauss above, we may draw up a basic
family structure with brother and sister at level 1, who both have father at
level 2, and relate to him through the relationships father-son and father-
daughter. The object father at level 2 is decomposed into objects son and
daughter at level 1. We can easily imagine building upon this with a level
3 which we can call father's father or grandfather, such that relationships
between levels 3 and 2 again capture the father-son relationship while
those between levels 3 and 1 take on relationships grandfather-grandson
and grandfather-granddaughter.

Certainly societies are structured as Radcliffe-Brown suggested, and as
well according to age, gender, hunting prowess, ceremonial knowledge
(all this set within the DMP at first), economic inequalities, political
inequalities, occupational diversity, religious status (all more prominent
as we head to VBH social forms).

Now, back to the larger issue of state variables. One thing to notice, following writers like Cowgill and Hardesty, is that technological variables sit among the state variables. In such schemes they are no longer linked with energy harnessed as independent variables in the manner of White's relation (4.2). They have a much more logical place as helping define a social form's state at any given time.

The state variables in some way *work* to bring about energy harnessing. To the extent that the s_i may concern individuals or groups we see them as capable of doing work, which in turns produces energy. Does this sound familiar? To answer that while exploring what it might mean, let us return momentarily, for analogy, to some basic physics. There work W is defined as the notion of moving a point of a force F through a distance d. That is,

$$W = Fd.$$

Then from Newton's second law we obtain

$$W = mad$$

where m is some mass and a the acceleration it attains under the force. But basic mechanics tells us that as we move such a mass along such a distance we have a starting velocity v_1 at the beginning and a final velocity v_2 at the end, according to the relation

$$d = \frac{\left(v_2^2 - v_1^2\right)}{2a}$$

where all symbols are as before; then

$$W = \frac{mv_2^2}{2} - \frac{mv_1^2}{2}$$

meaning that the work done in the system W is equal to the change in energy (recall the high school formula for kinetic energy: $1/2\,mv^2$). And as we acknowledge from (4.3) that such energy is a function of the state variables of the system, we see that the change in energy harnessed in any such situation will be a function of the work done by the system as an outcome of the structure of the state variables. That is

$$\Delta E = f(W) \tag{4.4}$$

where ΔE represents change in kinetic energy. To gain a better feel for what is implied by equations (4.3) and (4.4), let us continue with the physics analogy. Power in physics is defined as the rate of doing work. Let's call power V for argument's sake; then

$$V = W/t$$

where t is time. But this definition of power gives a beautiful analogy for social change and the social and political power caught up in that. For surely social and political power is related to the ability of some individual or group or class to demand, cajole, plead, that others do work on his/ their behalf or the behalf of the society. That is to say, the rate of doing work in such social contexts is directly attributable to the social power deployed to bring it about. The more social and political power brought to bear, the more work done by the society. In fact Harris (1975:397) tells us almost exactly that: power in human affairs "consists of the ability to control energy." To control energy in this way, he continues, "is to possess the means for making, moving, shaping, and destroying minerals, vegetables, animals, and people" (Harris 1975:397).

So continuing on with the elementary physical analogy from above, how might we characterise this social and political power? I suggest we look to social structure (above) which gives the hint that we can deploy as key variable an old friend from chapter 3: hierarchy.

Hierarchy provides us with a neat way of thinking about social and political power, and thence gives us a clear relation to work done and ultimately to the energy harnessed by the society. Which is all to say (4.4) becomes

$$\Delta E = f(h).$$ (4.5)

Energy harnessed by a society is a function of the hierarchy present in the society. To understand just how E depends on h, we can make this more useful, in similar fashion to methods employed in chapter 3, by expanding this function as a power series in the form of a Taylor expansion. Neglecting terms of low parsimony (Hutchinson 1978:2-3) as is usual, and expressing the change in energy harnessed against time, we see that in the limit as $\Delta t \to 0$ (4.5),takes the form of a rate of change of energy harnessing,

$$\frac{dE}{dt} = rE$$

which in turn provides the solution

$$E = e^{rt}$$ (4.6)

where e is what is known as the base of natural logarithms; an infinite non-repeating decimal that is known to hundreds of thousands of decimal places; the first few digits are

$$e = 2.71828...$$

(Simmons 1996:260). The intrinsic rate of growth is r.

So it appears that while Leslie White was correct in recognizing that energy harnessed produced goods and services, when we examine the issue slightly more closely, we are able to see energy harnessed, not as the key causal variable in social and cultural change that White judged it to be. Rather we see energy harnessed as a dependent variable. I have also suggested that it goes as a function of hierarchy, which in turn is itself characteristic of the set of state variables.

It will prove convenient to generalise (4.6) so that the shape of the curve fits more closely with known data patterns and gives us our independent variable of interest. If we let $e = b$, $r = c$, and $t = h$, the relation between the two variables is given by

$$E = ab^{hc} \qquad\qquad (4.7)$$

where h is the hierarchy index, and a, b and c are constants ($0 < a < 1$, $b > 1$, $0 < c < 1$). The values a and c are inserted to set the shape of the function by compression and stretching of the standard exponential function $f(x) = b^x$, shrinking it down towards the x-axis, and stretching it to the right (i.e. the positive direction of the x-axis) respectively. Note that as these two constants merely do shrinking and stretching jobs, the recovery of h means it has to be a substitute for t. This in turn shows the important result (4.7) that energy harnessed depends only on hierarchy.

It should come as no surprise to see that equations (4.6) and (4.7) take the form they do: an exponential function. Because from what little we know empirically about the history of state variables over time in social and cultural change, exponential functions loom large, particularly since the onset of agriculture. Probably the classic case of this is population growth. For population size would be a significant state variable in any social form, while its proposed change over the span of hominid evolution, especially where there are data available historically recorded or estimable in more recent times, is seen to be exponential (Hardesty 1971:177; Kleinman 1981:13-14; Gowlett 1984:196; Lambert 1987:214-215; most of whom to some extent, for the deep past at least, follow Deevey 1960). The data that give rise to these curves are all of reasonable fit to the shrunk and stretched general function (4.7).

However, we need to take heed of Hardesty's (1971) warning that there are a few basic patterns of human population growth. One of these is the so-called "J-shaped curve" of boom and bust: the population grows fast at first approximating an exponential growth pattern, but then crashes to a much smaller size (Hardesty 1971:177-178). As a consequence of societal collapse, this would fit with what I have argued above, whereby collapse emerges from the initial origin theory for VBH societies, as a predicted outcome.

Another set of state variables of interest relates to the exponential growth of technology – or more circumspectly, certain technologies – according to Moore's Law. This law states that at least during its period of empirical measurement from the 1960s through about year 2000, the number of transistors capable of being placed on a computer chip, doubled every eighteen months. This in turn provides a measure of how much computation can be performed; revealing an exponential increase over time in computing power (Ali Nouri & Chyba 2008:450). Moore's Law is now generalised to various aspects of exponential growth in technologies such as telecommunications and mechanical miniaturization (Hughes 2008:79).

Summary & Conclusions

In this chapter I have presented a brief outline of the main knowledge we have of VBH societies together with a theory for how they may have originated courtesy of structural changes in various DMP societies which gave rise to what I term Rogue Individuals. These in turn took hold of the newly developing economies and helped create VBH societies through appropriation of surpluses, establishment of armies and bureaucracies which shored up their developing power bases, introduced – with their allies and cohorts of followers, taxation, national religions and the full blown structure of the city state.

I then showed how mathematically we could expect the kind of theory I introduced to account for origins, to contain within itself a prediction of ultimate collapse. For these newly establishing and established systems are mostly unstable in their structures.

Finally I addressed the relation due to Leslie White that claims social evolution occurs in response to energy harnessing in any given social form. I showed that the White relation $E \times T \rightarrow P$ could be thought of as $P = f(E,T)$. I argued that for n state variables, s_i, the energy harnessed in a society has to be seen as a function of those state variables, such that $E = f(s_1, s_2, s_3, ...s_n)$. That is, the state variables in some way *work* to bring about energy harnessing. Hence the change in energy is seen as the change in work done, which is power. By the analogy with physical power we can see social power in action here bringing about the capacity to get work done. Then if that social power is seen as deriving from hierarchy, stratification within the society, we arrive at an equation which shows that the change in energy harnessed is a function of hierarchy. That is, $\Delta E = f(h)$. Because that change in energy in the limit can be considered infinitesimally, we can write it as a differential equation of the form $\frac{dE}{dt} = rE$, which in turn has a solution $E = e^{rt}$, where e is the base of natural logarithms. I suggested that to provide good fit to available data this relation can be generalised to $E = ab^{hc}$, where h is hierarchy.

While White appears to have been perceptive and correct with his correlation of energy harnessed and goods and services produced, this last part of the chapter gives some further context to that. It takes the White relation to another more fundamental and perhaps more realistic level. Energy harnessed is to be seen as a dependent variable whose drivers are the state variables of a given society at one level, through which hierarchy is singled out at a more technical and detailed level of description as the key independent variable.

CHAPTER 5

Conclusions

Prostitution is unstoppable. In Walters (2013) I developed a theory to show this, one that fits with all known evidence and makes a prediction that can be tested by historians or fieldworking social scientists. Here in chapter 2 I re-visited that theory, as one end of my function for prostitution, beefing up the introductory bit that draws on what we can learn from entropy, and adding a couple of mathematical niceties that make the presentation a little more sophisticated.

Chapter 2 shows that prostitution will continue forever, unable to be stopped by social, cultural or political forces, at least in the long haul. With one caveat: it can of course be stopped by such natural phenomena as biological extinction or cosmological catastrophe. For then, all babies go out with the bathwater.

The theory proves to be a surprising and unexpected outcome of introducing a species concept into sex work research. Reference to bar girls, call girls, or temporary wives as particular species of prostitution or sex work allows the use of the most simple measure of ecological diversity: the total number of species S_T. So any jurisdiction in any given historical period can be characterised by the number of species of prostitution present in the society or some given social setting. This not only permitted development of the quantitative picture necessary for the theory, but also allowed the theory to be tested empirically by future investigative historians. They can search out the records for the period of communist suppression and supposed prohibition, to see if like Hershatter, they can find types (species) of altered and adapted sex work continuing on despite the best efforts of a regime in denial.

In Walters (2013) I stressed that amid all the bright lights and glamour of theory, the implications are nevertheless extremely grounded and pragmatic. They are principally that prostitution can continue as an industry content in the belief that despite the best efforts of gainsaying authorities, their livelihood potential will continue. I do so stress again here.

The power of this theory is that it gives a political confidence never before attained logically and deductively, except in hope and perhaps insightful opinion: that sex work can and will continue forever. Yes it will change over time. Yes it will adapt. But no amount of abolitionist activity, lobby group pressure, legislative changes, periods of policing enthusiasm, will stop it. Do-gooders have no chance; they will not win. They may as well give up and turn their energies and attention to some useful and positive activities. Prostitution will be the winner, and in a civilised world of the future, will prevail to the end.

Then I turned to the other end of the function: the beginnings of prostitution. No historic or ethnographic, much less archaeological literature reveals evidence for prostitution prior to the Recent development of VBH societies. Then when it does appear in those societies it is suddenly ubiquitous. Though first known written records of prostitution date to around 3000 years ago, appearing in the historical writings of Herodotus, it may be that the gap between onset of VBH social forms and prostitution is merely a function of the latter needing to await the invention of writing, or writing on durable materials, to have its initial presence recorded for posterity.

Set theory was introduced to describe the beginnings of VBH lifeways via what I term the VBH set. This is found to characterise social history nicely. It shows for example, attributes of social structure dropping out of use or relevance over time, often as a result of being replaced by new forms. Particular use is made of what is known in set theory as the von Neumann constructible universe. This fits with the facts as it shows that varied cultures were free to pick and choose their own attributes, making them vastly diverse over time and space. This aspect of the theory also suggests that the general picture of nearly six million years of hunting and gathering is a tapestry of cumulative cultural pattern.

However, there is no implication here of progress, or that each and every culture is required to pass along the same linear path. Rather, the theory carries implications for the broad sweep of global culture. History and theory are aligned: things change over time, with a general human cumulative accretion of cultural traits.

Another feature of this part of the theory is that there is no going back. As with a cumulative collection of additive sets, addition of culture traits in general does not change direction, there is no reversion. Where a cultural trait is withdrawn from a social structure, where there is a subtraction, an abandonment, equivalence holds good, such that there is no structural reversion.

With VBH societies we see the addition of what I refer to as the VBH set. This is the set of sets that define VBH societies as a completely new phenomenon on planet Earth. Never before in the history of our world or the evolution of life on it has anything like it occurred. The VBH set contains elements of the kind: {king, court, bureaucracy, army, class, appropriated surplus, writing, numeracy, ... prostitution}.

Then I took another theoretical step, to consider history as a power series. That is, to consider some historical variable of interest which I called z. As we would expect for history, z is changing over time. I then suggested another variable of interest which depends on z and changes in accord with it, which I called $f(z)$. That is, some function of z. Because that's what this book and the theory are about, this latter variable I said we should call prostitution.

For our social variable z and the function, prostitution, $f(z)$, every time there is change we sum over history such that for all absolute values of $z < r$ the series settles down to a convergent value, a limiting value. Thus we see the situation of the DMP, where the system settled in every historical period without prostitution. Or perhaps there might have even been considerations for getting prostitution going, but these were rejected and the somewhat conservative social system settled back down to the steady as you go situation of traditional history. Then we see a radical break in history where suddenly, sometime – I suggest in the Holocene - we find prostitution extant in VBH societies. In this theoretical view, the historical sum of events has busted loose, diverged, brought on something completely new. This describes the historical record of prostitution, as far as it is currently known, neatly and exactly.

The theory leads to a pair of predictions. Firstly, as divergent power series sum to infinity, there is an immediate interpretation possible that suggests once prostitution is introduced, invented, got going, it is thereafter headed for infinity; it is unstoppable. Thus this part of the theory predicts the same conclusion reached by different theoretical means in chapter 2. This is not only confirming, but pleasing.

Secondly, for any given transition from a DMP society to a VBH one, there will exist a value of hierarchy $h = \lambda_i h_0$, where λ_i are some arbitrary coefficients which relate hierarchy in one kind of society to hierarchy in another kind of society. This is a first attempt at some sort of precision. Even though the coefficients remain arbitrary, to be determined, this potentially allows for more precise definition.

The transition from DMP to VBH society is characterised by a change in wealth distribution that goes from an approximately egalitarian distribution of resources throughout the society to one that has an appropriation parameter which characterizes its wealth distribution. I noted that the comparison of spread of wealth in the two societies is notionally observed by some fraction of wealth (which we can assume to be linked with some measure of power and prestige) per person, which when scanned across the entire probability distribution is what can be seen intuitively as a measure of hierarchy, h.

Having derived hierarchy h as a key independent variable in DMP to VBH social change, I then presented an index for in order for it to be a practical variable of use. The index allows calculation of h for various social forms. The method thus links us back to set theory. After that I gave a simple numerical example to show how such an index works for various hypothetical societies, both DMP and VBH.

Then the chapter switched to history, principally the accounts of prostitution from the time when writing comes into the archaeological record. I provided a set of quotes and references from Herodotus, writing of the Greek world in the period 3000 to about 2400 years ago. These were augmented by a small number of other sources as well. The major outcome of my examination of this work is to conclude that from about 3000 BP at least, there is a strong presence of prostitution in temples, with sex work also practised more secularly in brothels.

The final section of the chapter discusses the implications of this historical finding for what might be found archaeologically. A prediction is arrived at that prostitution began some 7000 years or so ago with the onset of VBH societies, and that with luck and appropriate variables examined by archaeologists, its presence might be detectable in the ruins of ancient sites from this time.

In chapter 4 I showed that the theory has implications for certain long standing issues in archaeology and anthropology: the origin and development of VBH societies; the collapse of many of them; and the relation between energy harnessed and social evolution, as articulated by Leslie White.

I developed a theory for how VBH societies may have originated. This relied on structural changes in various DMP societies that gave rise to what I term Rogue Individuals. Such individuals, embodying the collective, took control of rapidly developing economies and helped create VBH societies through appropriation of surpluses, and establishment of a power base of follower supporters. Eventually this would lead to new laws, state religion, armies, bureaucracies, taxation, intensified warfare, large scale irrigation systems, and the full blown structure of the city state.

I then pointed out that the mathematics of the kind of theory I introduced to account for origins, contains within itself a prediction of ultimate collapse. For these newly establishing and established systems are mostly unstable in their structures.

Finally, energy harnessed emerges as a dependent variable whose drivers are the state variables of a given society at one level, through which hierarchy is singled out at a more technical and detailed level of description as the key independent variable.

References

Adams, Fred C. & Gregory Laughlin 1997. A dying universe: the long-term fate and evolution of astrophysical objects. *Reviews of Modern Physics* 69(2):337-372.

Ali Nouri & Christopher F.Chyba 2008. Biotechnology and biosecurity. In Nick Bostrom & Milan M.Circovic (Editors) *Global Catastrophic Risks*, pp.450-480. Oxford: Oxford University Press.

Andaya, Barbara Watson 1998. From temporary wife to prostitute: sexuality and economic change in early modern Southeast Asia. *Journal of Women's History* 9(4):11-35.

Arnold, Vladimir I. 2004. *Catastrophe Theory*. Third Edition. Berlin: Springer-Verlag.

Atkins, Peter 2010. *The Laws of Thermodynamics: A Very Short Introduction*. Oxford: Oxford University Press.

Barrow, John D. & Frank J. Tipler 1986. *The Anthropic Cosmological Principle*. Oxford: Oxford University Press.

Beattie, John 1964. *Other Cultures: Aims, Methods and Achievements in Social Anthropology*. London: Routledge & Kegan Paul.

Binford, Lewis R. 1968. Post-Pleistocene adaptations. In S.R.Binford & L.R.Binford (Editors) *New Perspectives in Archaeology*. Chicago: Aldine.

Boas, Franz 1960 [1928]. *Anthropology and Modern Life*. New York: Dover.

Bohm, David & F.David Peat 1987. *Science, Order & Creativity*. London: Routledge.

Burn, A.R. 1988. Introduction. In *Herodotus: The Histories*. London: Penguin.

Chartrand, Gary 1985. *Introductory Graph Theory*. New York: Dover.

Chin Sung Chung 1995. Korean women drafted for military sexual slavery by Japan, In Keith Howard (Editor) *True Stories of the Korean Comfort Women*, pp.11-30. London: Cassell.

Cirkovic, Milan M. 2005. Permanence – an adaptationist solution to Fermi's paradox? *Journal of the British Interplanetary Society* 58:62-70.

Cirkovic, Milan M. 2008. Observation selection effects and global catastrophic risks. In Nick Bostrom & Milan M. Circovic (Editors) *Global Catastrophic Risks*, pp.120-145. Oxford: Oxford University Press.

Clark, Allan 1984. *Elements of Abstract Algebra*. New York: Dover.

Clifford, H.T. & W.Stephenson 1975. *An Introduction to Numerical Classification*. New York: Academic.

Cowgill, George L. 1975. On causes and consequences of ancient and modern population changes. *American Anthropologist* 77:505-525.

Deevey, E.S. 1960. The human population. *Scientific American* 203:194-204.

Diamond, Jared M. 1975. Assembly of species communities. In Martin L. Cody & Jared M.Diamond (Editors) *Ecology and Evolution of Communities*, pp.342-444. Cambridge, Mass.: Belknap of Harvard.

Diamond, Jared 1999. *Guns, Germs, and Steel: The Fates of Human Societies*. New York: Norton.

Douglas, Louise, Alan Roberts & Ruth Thompson 1988. *Oral History: A Handbook.* Sydney: Allen & Unwin.

Evans-Pritchard, E.E. 1974 [orig.1940] *The Nuer: A Description of the Modes of Livelihood and Political Institutions of a Nilotic People.* Oxford: Oxford University Press.

Fagan, Brian M. 1977. *People of the Earth: An Introduction to World Prehistory.* Second Edition. Boston: Little, Brown and Co.

Farley, Stanley J. 1993. *Partial Differential Equations for Scientists and Engineers.* New York: Dover.

Foley, Robert 1995. *Humans Before Humanity.* Oxford: Blackwell.

Goodall, Richard 1995. *The Comfort of Sin: Prostitutes & Prostitution in the 1990s.* Folkestone, UK: Renaissance Books.

Gowlett, John 1984. *Ascent to Civilization: The Archaeology of Early Man.* London: Book Club Associates.

Gunderson, Lance H., Craig R.Allen & C.S.Holling (Editors) 2010. *Foundations of Ecological Resilience.* Washington: Island Press.

Hardesty, Donald L. 1977. *Ecological Anthropology.* New York: Wiley.

Hardy, G.H. 2008. *A Course of Pure Mathematics.* Centenary Edition. Cambridge: Cambridge University Press.

Harris, Marvin 1975. *Culture, People, Nature: An Introduction to General Anthropology.* New York: Crowell.

Harris, Marvin 1979. *Cultural Materialism: The Struggle for a Science of Culture.* New York: Vintage.

Herodotus 1988. *Herodotus: The Histories.* London: Penguin.

Hershatter, Gail 1997. *Dangerous Pleasures: Prostitution and Modernity in Twentieth-Century Shanghai.* Berkeley: University of California Press.

Hicks, George 1997. *The Comfort Women: Japan's Brutal Regime of Enforced Prostitution in the Second World War.* New York: Norton.

Holling, C.S. 2010a. Resilience and stability of ecological systems. In Lance H.Gunderson, Craig R.Allen & C.S.Holling (Editors) *Foundations of Ecological Resilience*, pp. 19-49. Washington: Island Press.

Holling, C.S. 2010b. Engineering resilience versus ecological resilience. In Lance H.Gunderson, Craig R.Allen & C.S.Holling (Editors) *Foundations of Ecological Resilience*, pp. 51-66. Washington: Island Press.

Holling, C.S. 2010c. The resilience of terrestrial ecosystems: local surprise and global change. In Lance H.Gunderson, Craig R.Allen & C.S.Holling (Editors) *Foundations of Ecological Resilience*, pp. 67-118. Washington: Island Press.

Hughes, James J. 2008. Millennial tendencies in responses to apocalyptic threats. In Nick Bostrom & Milan M.Circovic (Editors) *Global Catastrophic Risks*, pp.73-90. Oxford: Oxford University Press.

Hutchinson, G.Evelyn 1978. *An Introduction to Population Ecology*. New Haven: Yale University Press.

Johnson, Gregory A. 1987. The changing organization in Uruk administration on the Susiana Plain. In *The Archaeology of Western Iran*, F.Hole (Editor). Washington DC: Smithsonian Institution Press.

Karnani, Mahesh, Kimmo Paakkonen & Arto Annila 2009. The physical character of information. *Proceedings of the Royal Society A* 465:2155-2175.

Kleinman, David 1981. *Human Adaptation and Population Growth: A Non-Malthusian Perspective*. Montclair, NJ: Allanheld, Osmun & Co.

Lam Thi Minh Nhuong & Ian Walters 2011. *Minh's Story: A Conversation*. Darwin: Historical Society of the Northern Territory.

Lambert, David 1987. *The Cambridge Guide to Prehistoric Man*. Cambridge: Cambridge University Press.

Levi-Strauss, Claude 1968. *Structural Anthropology*. Harmondsworth: Penguin.

Lienhardt, Godfrey 1966. *Social Anthropology*. London: Oxford University Press.

Ludwig, D., D.D.Jones & C.S.Holling 2010. Qualitative analysis of insect outbreak systems: the Spruce Budworm and Forest. In Lance H.Gunderson, Craig R.Allen & C.S.Holling (Editors) *Foundations of Ecological Resilience*, pp. 395-421. Washington: Island Press.

MacArthur, John W. 1975. Environmental fluctuations and species diversity. In Martin L. Cody & Jared M.Diamond (Editors) *Ecology and Evolution of Communities*, pp.74-80. Cambridge, Mass.: Belknap of Harvard.

Magurran, Anne E. 2004. *Measuring Biological Diversity*. Malden, MA: Blackwell.

May, Robert M. 1974. *Stability and Complexity in Model Ecosystems*. Princeton: Princeton University Press.

May, Robert M. 1975. Patterns of species abundance and diversity. In Martin L. Cody & Jared M.Diamond (Editors) *Ecology and Evolution of Communities*, pp.81-120. Cambridge, Mass.: Belknap of Harvard.

May, Robert M. 1978. The evolution of ecological systems. In *Evolution*, pp.80-90. (A Scientific American book) San Francisco: Freeman.

Mendelson, Bert 1990. *Introduction to Topology*. Third Edition. New York: Dover.

Pasuk Phongpaichit & Sungsidh Piriyarangsan 1994. *Corruption and Democracy in Thailand*. Chiang Mai: Silkworm.

Penrose, Roger 2004. *The Road to Reality: A Complete Guide to the Laws of the Universe*. New York: Vintage.

Priest, Graham 2000. *Logic: A Very Short Introduction*. Oxford: Oxford University Press.

Radcliffe-Brown, A.R. 1979 [orig.1952]. *Structure and Function in Primitive Society*. London: Routledge & Kegan Paul.

Reid, Anthony 1993a. *Southeast Asia in the Age of Commerce 1450-1680: Volume One: The Lands Below the Winds*. New Haven: Yale University Press.

Reid, Anthony 1993b. *Southeast Asia in the Age of Commerce 1450-1680: Volume Two: Expansion and Crisis*. New Haven: Yale University Press.

Rosenlicht, Maxwell 1968. *Introduction to Analysis*. New York: Dover.

Sahlins, Marshall 1974. *Stone Age Economics*. London: Tavistock.

Sahlins, Marshall 1976. *Culture and Practical Reason*. Chicago: University of Chicago Press.

Sahlins, Marshall 2000a. Introduction. In *Culture in Practice: Selected Essays*, pp.9-32. New York: Zone Books.

Sahlins, Marshall 2000b. The sadness of sweetness; or, the native anthropology of Western cosmology. In *Culture in Practice: Selected Essays*, pp.527-583. New York: Zone Books.

Sahlins, Marshall 2000c. What is anthropological enlightenment? Some lessons of the twentieth century. In *Culture in Practice: Selected Essays*, pp.501-526. New York: Zone Books.

Said, Edward W. 1994. *Representations of the Intellectual*. London: Vintage.

Scheffer, Marten 2009. *Critical Transitions in Nature and Society*. Princeton: Princeton University Press.

Schneider, Hans & George Phillip Barker 1973. *Matrices and Linear Algebra*. Second Edition. New York: Dover.

Scott, George Ryléy 1996 [1968]. *The History of Prostitution*. Twickenham, Middlesex: Senate.

Service, Elman R.1971. *Cultural Evolutionism: Theory in Practice*. New York: Holt, Rinehart & Winston.

Shannon, Claude E. & Warren Weaver 1998 [1949]. *The Mathematical Theory of Communication.* Urbana: University of Illinois Press.

Silk, Joseph 1980. *The Big Bang: The Creation and Evolution of the Universe.* San Francisco: W.H.Freeman.

Simmons, George F. 1996. *Calculus with Analytic Geometry.* Second Edition. New York: McGraw-Hill.

Sinha, Indra 1993. *Tantra: The Search for Ecstasy.* London: Hamlyn.

Sterling, Mary Jane 2009. *Linear Algebra for Dummies.* Hoboken, NJ: Wiley.

Swenson, R. & M.T.Turvey 1991. Thermodynamic reasons for perception-action cycles. *Ecological Psychology* 3(4):317-348.

Thom, Rene 1989 [1972]. *Structural Stability and Morphogenesis: An Outline of a General Theory of Models.* Westview Press Advanced Book Classics.

Toynbee, Arnold 1947. *A Study of History.* New York: Oxford.

Walters, Ian 2013. *Sex Work in Vietnam.* amazon Kindle Direct Publishing [ebook].

Warren, James Francis 1993. Ah Ku *and* Karayuki-san: *Prostitution in Singapore 1870-1940.* Singapore: Oxford University Press.

Wenke, Robert J., 1999. *Patterns in Prehistory: Humankind's First Three Million Years.* 4th Edition. New York: Oxford.

White, Leslie A. 2007 [1959]. *The Evolution of Culture: The Development of Civilization to the Fall of Rome.* Walnut Creek, Ca.: Left Coast Press.

Wright, Henry T. 1987. The Susiana Hinterlands during the era of primary state formation. In *The Archaeology of Western Iran*, F.Hole (Editor). Washington DC: Smithsonian Institution Press.

Wurtz, Peter & Arno Annila 2008. Roots of diversity relations. *Journal of Biophysics*, Article ID 654672, 8 pages, doi:10,1155/2008/654672.

INDEX

Andaya, Barbara Watson 106

Big Man (BM) 63,132,134-5,139-
40,144-5,148-9,153
bedroom sex 5,104-7
Boltzmann Law 3,20

catastrophe (theory) 12-4
civilization, see VBH societies
complex societies, see VBH
societies

discontinuity 12-4,57,110,133
diversity (biological, species)
3,30,35,39
Domestic Mode of Production
(DMP societies) 43,45,47-
9,52-7,63,71-8,83-91,105,108-
12,128,132-6,138-42,148-
9,158,162,167,174-5

Eddington, Arthur 20
Egyptologists 6
entropy 3,16,18-21,31,37-8

Fermi's dilemma (Fermi's
paradox) 46-7
function(s) 1,11-3

Herodotus 5,91-101,113,175
Hershatter, Gail 2,24,36
Hierarchy 5, 9-10, 44,75-
91,112,120,143,162,165-6,168-
9,174,176
Holocene 5,6,9,42,52,106,127,173

information theory 3,20-1,31-3,38

Johnson, Gregory 10,120

Levi-Strauss (Claude) 13,161-2

Moore's Law 167

Newtonian caveat 4,37-8
noisy channel 3,32-3

oldest profession 4,48

Radcliffe-Brown (A.R.) 13,161-2
resilience theory 13
Rigveda, see Vedic
Rogue Individual(s) (RI)
11,65,135-6,140-50,153,168,175

Sahlins, Marshall
43,53-6,83,132-4,141-2
Second Law of Thermodynamics
3,20,33
Shannon, Claude 3,31-3,35
signal 3,33

singularity theory, see catastrophe
social contract 50
species concept 24-31,39,170-1

taxonomy 21-31
Thom, Rene 12-3

VBH (Very Big Hierarchy)
societies 10-1,16,18,41,43,45,48,52-
3,56-8,62-6,73-8,86-
91,96,101,104,108-15,118-21,124-
7,129,132,136,138-42,144-6,149-
51,153,162,167-8,172-5
Vedic (Rigveda) 100

White, Leslie 6,8,9,102-
3,115,151,154-6,159-60,166,168-9
writing 117-9,124

About the Author

Dr Ian Walters studied ecology (zoology) and anthropology (including his PhD in archaeology) at University of Queensland, and mathematics through MIT's (Massachusetts Institute of Technology's) Open Courseware program. Following a career teaching and researching in Australian universities, he now lives and writes in Asia. He is the author of *Dasher Wheatley & Australia in Vietnam*, *Minh's Story*, and *Sex Work in Vietnam*, as well as the novels *The Theory of Relativity*, *Hanh Dien* and *King of the Woods*.

Printed in the United States
By Bookmasters